A Nun, a Convent, and the German Occupation of Belgium

Also by Rene Kollar

Westminster Cathedral: From Dream to Reality

*The Return of the Benedictines to London: The History
of Ealing Abbey from 1896 to Independence*

*Abbot Aelred Carlyle, Caldey Island, and the
Anglo-Catholic Revival in England*

*A Universal Appeal: Aspects of the Revival of Monasticism
in the West in the 19th and Early 20th Centuries*

*Searching for Raymond: Anglicanism, Spiritualism,
and Bereavement between the Two World Wars*

*A Foreign and Wicked Institution?
The Campaign against Convents in Victorian England*

A Nun, a Convent, and the German Occupation of Belgium

Mother Marie Georgine's Diary of World War I

EDITED BY
Rene Kollar

PICKWICK *Publications* · Eugene, Oregon

A NUN, A CONVENT, AND THE GERMAN OCCUPATION
OF BELGIUM
Mother Marie Georgine's Diary of World War I

Pickwick Publications
An Imprint of Wipf and Stock Publishers
199 W. 8th Ave., Suite 3
Eugene, OR 97401

www.wipfandstock.com

PAPERBACK ISBN: 978-1-4982-9892-6
HARDCOVER ISBN: 978-1-4982-9894-0
EBOOK ISBN: 978-1-4982-9893-3

Cataloguing-in-Publication data:

Names: Kollar, Rene Matthew, 1947–.

Title: A nun, a convent, and the German occupation of Belgium : Mother Marie Georgine's diary of World War I / Rene Kollar.

Description: Eugene, OR: Pickwick Publications, 2016.

Identifiers: ISBN 978-1-4982-9892-6 (paperback) | ISBN 978-1-4982-9894-0 (hardcover) | ISBN 978-1-4982-9893-3 (ebook).

Subjects: LCSH: World War I, 1914–1918—History. | Monasticism and religious orders—History—20th century. | Women—Religious life. | Convents & nuns.

Classification: D542 V46 2016 (print) | D541 (ebook).

Manufactured in the U.S.A.   12/02/16

To the students of Saint Vincent College

Contents

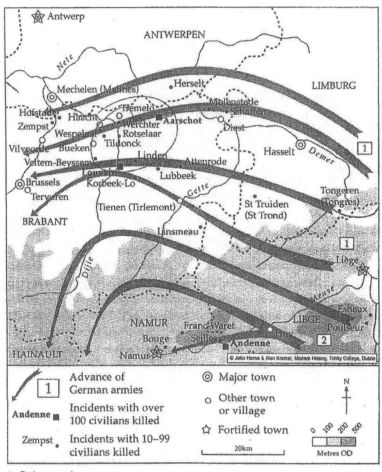

1 Advance of German armies	◎ Major town	N ↑
Andenne ■ Incidents with over 100 civilians killed	○ Other town or village	
Zempst . Incidents with 10–99 civilians killed	☆ Fortified town	0 100 200 500
	20km	Metres OD

4   Brabant province

Brabant Province, August 1914. Map drawn by Matthew Stout, taken from John Horne and Alan Kramer, *German Atrocities, 1914: A History of Denial* (London: Yale University Press, 2001).

The Convent at Tildonk

Acknowledgments

I CAME ACROSS THIS important typewritten copy of Mother Marie Georgine's hand written letters assembled in the form of a diary by accident. During the summer of 2014, I attended a conference on the outbreak of World War I in London and I visited the Imperial War Museum (IWM). My current research deals with convent life, and I searched the IWM catalogue to see if it contained any interesting material on sisterhoods and the war years, and I was surprised to find a typed copy of Mother Marie Georgine's diary with a description of its contents. The staff of the IWM was very helpful in answering my questions dealing with the diary and providing me with a photocopy. I contacted Sr. Kathleen Colmer, OSU, Provincial of the English Province, about whom to contact concerning the copyright and permission to publish the diary, and she directed me to the Ursulines of Tildonk in Belgium. I received an encouraging reply from the General Superior, Ursuline Sisters of Tildonk, Sr. Bimla Minj, OSU. She told me that she had a conversation with Provincial Superior, Sr Ann Cuppens, OSU, who was also very positive about my plans to publish Mother Marie Georgine's diary. Sister Ann and I were exchanging emails about this project when I was saddened to learn about her sudden death in May 2015. I appreciate very much her support and interest in my project. Sr. Bimla then sent me the name and the email address of the current Provincial Superior, Sr. Hildegarde Verherstraeten, OSU, and soon afterwards I received the information I requested, namely, biographical information on Mother Marie Georgine, pictures of her and the convent at Tildonk, and information about the school, from Sr. Bernadette Uytterhoeven, OSU. Sr. Hildegarde, holder of the copyright, also gave me permission to publish the diary. I greatly appreciate the help and encouragement of these Ursuline Sisters. Barbara Hester also supplied me with valuable information and material about Mother Marie Georgine, her great grandaunt. She believes that Mother Marie Georgine wrote these letters, which appear in the form of a diary, to her brother, Cecil Holt. I am very thankful for her help and assistance.

Several people at Saint Vincent Archabbey and College have been instrumental in this project. Archabbot Douglas Nowicki, OSB, has always encouraged and supported my research. Fr. François Diouf, OSB, gave me valuable insights into the meaning of several French words, and Fr. Brian Boosel, OSB, took time out from writing his doctoral dissertation to read the diary and to comment on, and at times, correct my translations of French into English. Monks of the Archabbey and my colleagues in the School of Humanities and Fine Arts encouraged me as my work progressed. Ms. Marsha Kush, Assistant to the Dean of the School of Humanities and Fine Arts, retyped the manuscript which I received from the Imperial War Museum and raised some important questions about spelling and consistency in this text. Finally, a Faculty Development Grant from the School of Humanities and Fine Arts, Saint Vincent College, helped to fund my trip to London in the summer of 2014.

Some remarks on my editing. I tried to remain faithful to the typed manuscript which I received from the IWM, especially the English spelling, punctuation, and designation of hours of the day, and made only a few changes when necessary or for consistency. I italicized the French words, added the appropriate accents, and provided the translation in brackets immediately following the French in the text the first time the word appears. Definitions of other words which may not be familiar to the reader and a short identification of several people were placed in brackets in the same manner. Mother Marie Georgine offered her own comments, and these appeared in parenthesis in the typewritten manuscript. I also italicized words or phrases which were underlined in the text. In respect to proper place names in Belgium, I did not deviate from Mother Marie Georgine's spelling, but corrected what appeared to be misspellings or typographical errors. "Thildonck" is the French spelling of the town, and "Tildonk" is the preferred Flemish spelling.

Rene Kollar

Introduction

SINCE 1839 AND THE Treaty of London, the neutral status of Belgium had been guaranteed. But because of its strategic geographical location, at the outbreak of World War I Germany quickly violated the neutrality of this small country to implement its Schlieffen Plan, an attempt to encircle France and eventually capture Paris. On August 4, 1914, German forces invaded Belgium and met with resistance which resulted in atrocities and acts of barbarism against its inhabitants and the destruction of town and cities.[1] According to Philip Jenkins, "At the height of their invasion in August and September of 1914, the Germans slaughtered six thousand civilians in Belgium and northern France, most (falsely) on the suspicion of being *francs-tireurs* (snipers) or saboteurs."[2] Nervous German soldiers responded to perceived threats of gunfire by destroying houses, taking hostages, and executing prisoners on the pretext of self-defense from snipers. They did not even spare the historic city of Louvain as the army advanced in August 1914. The invading troops "torched the library and its collection

1. See Horne and Kramer, *German Atrocities, 1914*; and Zuckerman, *The Rape of Belgium.*

2. Jenkins, *The Great and Holy War*, 37. For more information on *francs-tireurs* see Horne and Kramer, *German Atrocities, 1914*, 94–113. Jenkins also notes that "No side in this war had a monopoly of atrocities," e.g., the British use of dum-dum ammunition and the blockade of food supplies and the actions of the "massacres and ethnic cleansing, particularly of Poles and Jews in their western and border regions, which inflicted casualties far higher than anything the Germans ever caused in Belgium" (38–39).

of rare books and manuscripts, and soldiers carried out random mass shootings." Throughout the war years, Germany continued its harsh treatment of Belgium as it continued its military operations. Historians such as Paul Fussell, Martin Gilbert, Peter Hart, Max Hastings, Philip Jenkins, John Keegan, Lyn Macdonald, and Jay Winter have chronicled the events of World War I, but other accounts from unlikely sources also vividly describe life in occupied Belgium—the eyewitness reports of Roman Catholic nuns.

Diaries or recollections of nuns caught up in the events of World War I in Belgium became a popular vehicle to describe the sufferings of a neutral, Roman Catholic country invaded by an army which many viewed as hostile to Catholicism. An early account, *The Irish Nuns at Ypres: An Episode of the War*, written by the Irish Benedictine nun, Dame M. Columban, describes the experiences of her community at Ypres from August 1914 until the community relocated at St. Mary's Abbey in Oulton, England, at the end of the year.[3] The battle for Ypres had a great impact on the nuns, and the author recalls the brutish actions of the German troops, the famine, and the suffering of refugees fleeing the fighting. Describing the destruction and burning of the countryside and villages by the Germans and other atrocities, this Irish nun stated that "what moved us most was the account of the outrageous barbarities used upon women, even upon nuns."[4] However, despite "the danger and anxiety, we strove to keep up religious life, and the regular observances." England was the next stop for these Irish Benedictines after leaving Belgium, and after an uneventful journey to the French coast and channel crossing, these nuns travelled from London to Oulton in Staffordshire and eventually resettled in Ireland.

In another personal account, Sister Marie Antoine of the Convent of Mercy, Willebroeck, Belgium, wrote about her experiences during the early months of the German invasion and concluded her story with her arrival in America where she began seeking funds to repair her convent and the damages done to the order's

3. O'Brien, *The Irish Nuns at Ypres.*
4. Ibid., 37.

boarding school in Belgium. The peaceful, joyful atmosphere of summer 1914 contrasts sharply with the chaos of the early months of the war, in particular the destruction of Louvain, "the heart of Catholic Belgium, the principal place of her Christian educational institutions, and the seat of her missionary forces."[5] The carnage of the war, the care provided to the wounded by the Red Cross and the nuns, the sufferings of innocent civilians, and atrocities committed by the "Godless element in the German army, led on and sustained by equally Godless officers . . ." are subjects of the early stages of the German occupation. Her vivid descriptions of the nuns' work among the refugees, displaced families, and the wounded testify to the courage of these women. In October, Sister Marie Antoine and several other nuns departed from Belgium to England, where the generosity of the people toward the plight of Belgium impressed her, before she departed for America.

In some aspects, *The Little Nun: The Diary of One of Belgium's Unhappy Victims*[6] is very similar to the previous two works: the time frame is the initial months of the war; all three deal with the lives of nuns who experienced the horrors of the conflict and their heroic actions; and the authors describe the atrocities and barbaric actions of the invading Germans. Helpless civilians and Catholics are victims of Belgium's enemy. But *The Little Nun* differs from the other two journals in several ways. The saga of the sisters of Ypres and Willebroeck does not hide the names of the nuns or the locations associated with their experiences. The translator of *The Little Nun*, on the other hand, deals with his subject in a different manner. In the Preface, he states that it was the desire of the mother of the "Little Nun," who gave him the journal, not to mention the name of her daughter to avoid scandal and disgrace which might taint the family name because of the physical and mental torments this nun endured. For the same reason, all references to her religious community and locations in Belgium are also absent. The nuns from Ypres and Willebroeck found safety and the hope for a new life in England and America, while the third account of

5. Sister Marie Antoine, *From Convent to Conflict*, 65.

6. *The Little Nun*, 1916.

wartime Belgium and the life of the "Little Nun" end in a tragic note of despair. German atrocities certainly touched the lives of the Irish and Ypres nuns, but the brutalities and sufferings which the anonymous "Little Nun" personally suffered were both mental and physical abuse. *The Little Nun*, therefore, presents a more graphic account of the first months of the war and paints the Germans in the darkest light and attempts to elicit sympathy for the citizens of Belgium. Another diary written in the form of letters by Mother Marie Georgine, a member of the Ursuline convent at Tildonk, Belgium, is more inclusive. It covers the entire war period and deals with the military activities and atrocities, but also gives an insight into the daily life of this convent and its members and the manner in which these nuns reacted to the circumstances of an occupied Belgium.

The Ursulines at Tildonk, situated in Flemish Brabant approximately 34 kilometers from Brussels and 9 kilometers from Louvain, began their existence in the aftermath of the French Revolution. French anti-religious policies closed Catholic churches, convents, and monasteries and passed harsh laws discriminating against Catholicism. Violence often followed, and nuns and clergy were persecuted and killed. The founder of the Ursuline Sisters of Tildonk, John Cornelius Lambertz (1785–1869) was born in Hoogstraten, Belgium, during this chaotic period.[7] After his ordination in 1812, Lambertz was assigned to a parish in Tildonk, and he recognized the necessity of educating young girls who lacked the financial means to pursue schooling. The foundation of the school can be traced back to 1818 when three young women, Anna-Marie Van Groederbeek, Maria Van Ackerbrouck, and Catharina Van den Schriek, expressed their desire to Fr. Lambertz to pursue vocations as nuns. After a retreat conducted by this parish priest, these three women "offered themselves to the Lord" and began to live at the parish house as "Daughters of Saint Ursula." They chose to follow the traditions and goals of the Order of St. Ursula, founded

---

7. See Holemans, *The Curé of Thildonk*. This is an English version by Mother Mary Clare of a previously published French edition. See also http://osutildonk.com.

in 1535 by St. Angela Merici which emphasized the education of girls, which became a key element in Fr. Lambertz's original plans. The small community grew, and in 1832 it adopted the Rule of St. Augustine and Constitutions of the Ursuline Sisters of Bordeaux, and the Congregation of the Ursuline Sisters of Tildonk became a reality. Fr. Lambertz was now able to establish convents of the Ursuline Sisters of Tildonk in Belgium, the Netherlands, and Germany, and he opened schools for needy girls. Moreover, nuns from Tildonk were soon instrumental in establishing convents throughout the world.[8]

In addition to a commitment to educate young women at its boarding school, the convent at Tildonk demonstrated its concern for the poor and the refugee by welcoming nuns fleeing France as a result of the 1901 anti-Catholic Law of Association. By the outbreak of World War I, the convent at Tildonk had become recognized as an outstanding boarding school for girls with an international flavor. Because of its academic reputation and the opportunity to learn French, English families sent their daughters to be educated by the Ursulines at Tildonk. Art, music, dance, and needle work were also taught, and most girls remained at the school for the entire year. The English girls, it is reported, also liked to play cricket! And the tradition of caring for the destitute and homeless also continued. This provided the backdrop for Mother Marie Georgine's accounts of the convent during the occupation of Belgium by German forces during the war.

Isoline Jones, daughter of Charles Jones and Catherine Mandell and the youngest of ten children, was born on March 31, 1876, in Watford, England.[9] Religion played an important part in her life. Both her father and a brother, Cecil Holt, were Church of England

8. See the above histories for the growth of this order and foundations which chose to join or established other provinces.

9. Details of Mother Marie Georgine's life, her photograph, and information on the history of the school, which appears above in the Introduction, were supplied by Sister Bernadette Uytterhoeven, OSU, of the Ursuline Sisters of Tildonk, Belgium. Barbara Hester also supplied me with valuable information about Mother Marie Georgine, her great grandaunt, from family records and from the Tildonk archives.

vicars. At the age of 16, she arrived at the convent school at Tildonk in October 1892. Isoline left the boarding school on January 10, 1894, but the life of the Ursuline Sisters must have had a great influence on her. When she turned 21, she asked her father for permission to convert to Roman Catholicism, and Isoline was baptized on April 17, 1897, at the sisters' chapel at Tildonk.[10] But her spiritual journey did not end when she became a Catholic. Three years after her baptism Isoline decided to join the Ursulines. She became a postulant in 1900 and took the name of Marie Georgine of the Flagellation. She professed temporary vows as an Ursuline Sister on November 25, 1902, and on November 13, 1907, Mother Marie Georgine made perpetual vows as a member of the order. She spent her entire life as a religious working at the Tildonk convent. She instituted a shorthand typist course and taught English and Arithmetic to the students. The enrollment at the school suffered during the turmoil of World War I, and because of a lack of English students in 1917 she was assigned to care for the sick.

Mother Marie Georgine's letters, written in the form of a diary, give a vivid account of her activities during World War I, and an interesting piece of information about her life deals with an event reminiscent of August 1914: the invasion of Belgium by German troops at the outbreak of World War II. In 1914, Mother Marie Georgine remained at the convent, but as the Germans occupied Belgium in 1940 she accompanied the English students to safety across the Channel. In England, she probably visited the Ursuline Sisters located at Brentwood. There is no record of Mother Marie Georgine's eventual return to Tildonk or her life at the convent. On November 18, 1962, she celebrated her Diamond Jubilee to mark 60 years of religious life, and former students from England attended the festivities. Mother Marie Georgine became ill in early December, and on Christmas Day she was anointed, and she died on December 31, 1962. Although much of her life is

10. Isoline Jones was baptized as an Anglican on July 20, 1876, at St. Mary's, Watford, Hertford. Her Roman Catholic baptism at Tildonk was probably a conditional baptism, that is, when there is doubt or questions about the validity of a previous legitimate baptism. This is not rebaptism.

not documented, her diary gives an insight into her dedication to the Gospel and her life of service as an Ursuline Sister of Tildonk.

Portions of Mother Marie Georgine's diary have been published previously. *Women's Writing of the First World War: An Anthology* has a short entry from August 23, 1914, which gives an account about a search of the convent grounds by the Germans looking for concealed weapons or soldiers. Nothing was found.[11] *For King and Country: Voices from the First World War* contains Mother Marie Georgine's journal entry for November 24, 1914, and describes German atrocities including crucifixions.[12] Mother Marie Georgine's typewritten copy of her experiences can be found at the Imperial War Museum, London. By the time the diary begins on August 16, 1914, twelve days after the German invasion of Belgium, some of the students had fled, but others remained with the nuns. The first entries in her journal deal with the German advance on Antwerp, the plight of the refugees, the establishment of a field hospital for wounded Belgium soldiers, housing of German troops, and the arrival of General Hans Hartwig von Beseler and the Army General Staff [État Major] at the convent to direct the siege the city (September to October 1914). Mother Marie Georgine's recollections of the war years is a collection of letters in the form of a journal written to the author's family and friends, whom she identifies by their first names, which describe life at the Ursuline convent at Tildonk, and thus it offers valuable insights into the impact of the war on the convent, its school, and civilian life.[13] Her diary ends on December 15, 1918.

11. Smith, *Women's Writing of the First World War*, 45.

12. MacArthur, *For King and Country*, 52–53.

13. Another diary dealing with the Ursuline convent at Tildonk, described as the "Tildonk Diary," is in the Lucas Collection located in the Midlothian Council Archives in Scotland. The author is an anonymous woman, most likely a nun or student, living in the Tildonk convent. This journal begins on August 1, 1914, and concludes at the end of October 1914. Her descriptions of these early hectic months, which have been published online, are similar to those of Mother Marie Georgine but more succinct. See https://tildonkdiary.wordpress.com.

Mother Marie Georgine has written a superb narrative which captures the tensions which the nuns experienced throughout the war and their dealings with the German invaders who occupied their school and convent grounds for a time. The majority of the diary entries deal with the first two years of the war, but she also vividly describes the events of the final years. Mother Marie Georgine does not hide her emotions and feelings in her descriptions of the atrocities of the German soldiers committed against priests, nuns, and the people of Belgium. The care given by members of the convent to refugees and the wounded, the activities of numerous members of the Tildonk community and neighboring clergy during the occupation, and the daily life of the school are important aspects of her journal. Her discussions of the siege of Antwerp, the destruction of Louvain, and tragic events of the war which took place in several Belgium towns and villages will interest anyone interested in World War I, especially local Belgium history. Some entries are long, others brief, and substantial gaps of time occur between her accounts of convent life, but this does not interrupt the flow of her story.

Mother Marie Georgine's stories and vignettes about the life of the school at Tildonk and the impact of the war on convent life make for good reading, and her commentaries are not cold and impersonal. One comes to an appreciation of her personality and dedication to her religious vocation to service in the pages of this diary, and she identifies several members of the convent by name and shows how they coped with living in an occupied country. In addition to recounting encounters with anonymous German soldiers, two German Generals, von Beseler and Bissing, receive some attention. As the German occupation became more intolerable and the sufferings of Belgians became more pronounced, Cardinal Désiré Joseph Mercier, Archbishop of Malines and Primate of Belgium, wrote a Christmas Pastoral Letter in 1914, titled "Patriotism and Endurance," which was distributed throughout the country. Mother Marie Georgine refers to Mercier as the "Cardinal" and provides an excellent insight into this churchman's personality and courage and the reaction of the Germans to his challenging address to his countrymen and the world. The author's dedication to ministering to those harmed by the war and exposing the brutalities of the invading army are the main topics, but interesting anecdotes and examples of humor and wit about convent life are also present. Mother Marie Georgine's diary entries conclude in December 1918, for example, with a bit of sarcasm as she describes groups of German prisoners, often guarded by a single Belgium soldier, repairing destroyed railway lines: "That is tit for tat with a vengeance!"

Bibliography

Antoine, Sister Marie. *From Convent to Conflict: Or, A Nun's Account of the Invasion of Belgium.* Baltimore: Murphy, 1916.

Columban, Dame M. (D. M. C.). *The Irish Nuns at Ypres: An Episode of the War.* Edited by Barry R. O'Brien. London: Smith, Elder, 1915.

Holemans, F. *The Curé of Thildonk (Rev. J. C. M. Lambertz) 1785–1869.* Translated by Mother Mary Clare Holemans. London: Burns, Oates & Washbourne, 1933.

Horne, John, and Alan Kramer. *German Atrocities, 1914: A History of Denial.* New Haven: Yale University Press, 2001.

Jenkins, Philip. *The Great and Holy War: How World War I Became a Religious Crusade.* New York: HarperCollins, 2014.

The Little Nun: The Diary of One of Belgium's Unhappy Victims. Translated by E. A. London: Cassell, 1916.

MacArthur, Brian, ed. *For King and Country: Voices from the First World War.* London: Abacus, 2009.

Smith, Angela K., ed. *Women's Writing of the First World War.* Manchester: Manchester University Press, 2000.

Zuckerman, Larry. *The Rape of Belgium: The Untold Story of World War I.* New York: New York University Press, 2004.

1

August 16, 1914—December 20, 1914

Thildonck [Tildonk]. August 16, 1914.

YOUR LETTER WAS VERY welcome and by this time I hope you have received my first volume safely. This promises to be a second of the same description. I would address it to Dora [Mother Marie Georgine's sister] only there is no saying where she is or what has become of her at the present moment. I cannot understand how it is that you are all of you so easy in your minds about the 5 [members of Mother Marie Georgine's family] in Gy [Germany].[1] Violet is not much protection unless she is naturalised and I never heard that she was. Perhaps their numerous German friends will be a sufficient guarantee but with all the horrors one years of in the papers, I do not myself feel particularly reassured. However, there is no means of getting news so it is useless to worry. One can but hope for the best and pray. Whatever else we may have to complain of, we can hardly complain of monotony at present, nor shall we be able to I fear for a long time to come. I sent off your last letter on Monday and then I told you that we hoped to have an ambulance [a mobile field hospital]. These things do not seem to be managed here quite as in England judging from the papers. There were

---

1. Evelyn and Violet were Mother Marie Georgine's siblings. Violet married a Silesian, Franz Philip Kauffmann, and they had two children. Violet remained in Germany during the duration of the war.

pictures of people being practically turned out of their houses which were to be transformed into hospitals and their furniture stowed away in barns, etc. Here the enthusiasm is so great that everyone is volunteering. The bishops (or at any rate our Cardinal)[2] sent a circular letter to all the convents prescribing certain prayers and saying that if any were able to undertake an ambulance they were to let him know and he would make the necessary arrangements, the conditions being that there must be at least 3 certificated sick nurses in the house. We have four besides the sisters who usually look after the sick nuns and children so we immediately offered. Since then he has also asked convents to look after children left homeless by the war, but I don't fancy we shall do that just at present for the less children we have here the better as things stand. We immediately began our preparations and transformed the *petit pensionnat* [small boarding school] into a hospital. The *salle* [room, hall] makes a splendid ward and the classes have each four beds in for more serious cases. One room is a dispensary and so forth. M. le Directeur [manager, director] postponed the whole affair saying that it was quite premature as the authorisations had not arrived and putting it all down to feminine enthusiasm but we maintained that it was not the moment to begin when we had already sick men waiting in the house for beds and bandages. That same afternoon M. le Curé [parish priest] of Delle [neighboring parish to Tildonk] arrived with a company of men in his wake. Dirty, dusty, tired out men who had been patrolling the country all day in the broiling heat on the look out for spies. We put benches for them in front of the house and gave them food. Then he enquired if we could not tend to those who had broken down. One quite lame from too much marching, one with an awful throat, another with stitch [side cramp] and another quite prostrate with constant reaching. Of course we were only too pleased, and they were our first patients. Next day we received an alert in the afternoon that soldiers were coming to lodge in the village and that we

2. Désiré Joseph Mercier (1851–1926) became Archbishop of Malines in 1907 and was made a Cardinal in 1907. Mother Marie Georgine makes reference later to the Cardinal's Christmas 1914 Pastoral Letter.

should have to put up at least 800 here as well as the officers. You can imagine the excitement. There were to be 4000 of them in the village altogether, the 6th and 26th *de Ligne* from Antwerp. Towards four o'clock a soldier arrived to make arrangements. Finally arrived the men themselves. We have to send round to different farms for straw for them to sleep on. The whole of the *externat* [day school] (poor school)[3] was given up to them and there were men in all the classes [classrooms], besides which the corridor was full of them and in one class mattresses were put on the floor for what they call the *sous-officiers* [junior officers]. We should call them non-commissioned officers I suppose. Similarly the *salle des fêtes* [recreation area, social hall] (your swimming bath) and the other two huge *salles* were covered with straw and the men packed as tight as possible, still not room enough. Finally they went up on to the bridge as well and even into the corridor *des classes*. The officers slept in the rooms prepared with four beds to a room while the quite superior ones, general, colonel, etc., had the *chambres à loger* [guest rooms]. The farm was given over to the dogs and ammunitions especially the *mitrailleuses* [early type of machine gun] (I don't know the English for it but it has something to do with grape-shot). They were most interesting to see and one of the men showed me one completely and explained it as thoroughly as possible to a person quite ignorant of those matters. He showed me too the bands of grape shot and said that the *mitrailleuses* fired about 400–500 shot a minute killing a corresponding number of men if well directed. They are fixed in small carts drawn by dogs who seem to quite enjoy their functions. The great business of the men when they arrived was to get a good wash and to satisfy their demands; all the pails in the house were requisitioned in the farm yard, in the big ones' playground, and the poor school they were standing in crowds stripped to the waist having a good-swill. Oh, how grateful they were. The officers were offered baths and simply jumped at it so that the bath rooms were constantly occupied until past 11. They had numbers of men with them

3. Mother Marie Georgine's definition. Throughout the diary, the author's definitions or descriptions of French terms are presented in parentheses.

requiring attention so that the infirmary was regularly invaded. They had a military doctor and several Red Cross men with them but imagined that we had no provision for them as we were not flying a Red Cross flag. When they found the true state of affairs and that we only required the authorisation they took the law into their own hands. They went up to the top of the house by the big reservoir, and fixed up a huge flag themselves besides putting them at a window on each side of the house. As long as the soldiers were here I don't believe that the infirmarians got to bed at all. They looked after their own food and made themselves two kitchens one in the playground of the *externat* and one just outside the big ones' playground. They seemed to feel that they had fallen on their feet for once and profited of their opportunities. The sisters were up to unearthly hours of the night, washing their shirts, socks, etc., which were sights to behold. Then came trousers to be mended, etc., etc. Poor fellows, you should have seen the state they were in and such a mixture. Some of course were the rough common soldiers type but many were very much the reverse, the sons of wealthy people, accustomed at home to every luxury. Among the number were the brothers of two of our children and of one of the nuns (you can imagine her delight). There certainly was an alert of some sort or we should not have had them but everything is kept so dark that nobody knows anything. The soldiers have no idea where they are going or when or why and the officers themselves know very little more, just what is absolutely necessary for the time being. Most of them had seen no papers for days except those we gave them. They did not know how long they were to stay and were ready to leave at a moment's notice all the time they were here. A patrol slept outside on the grass all night and during the day they kept a look out on the roof by the reservoir. Aeroplanes were overhead constantly, some, no doubt were Belgian and French but I am certain some were Germans trying to find out what all those troops were doing here, and I fancy they thought so too but they had orders not to shoot at them. An old woman came and told one of the men that she had been stopped by a strange man on the road who asked her all sorts of questions and why the troops were here, where they are going, etc. They were off like a shot and caught the individual who naturally proved to be a spy. There was a plumber working in the roof of the *externat* and the foolish man had borrowed some opera glasses thinking he would amuse himself looking at the troops. He reckoned without his host for the soldiers very naturally took him for a spy and two officers were up on to the roof like lightning. He was searched then and there and pretty roughly handled. Poor man, he thought his last hour had come which indeed was nearly the case. He was hauled over to the hotel [civil authorities or Town Hall] and Rev. M. Gen. [Rev. Mother General] had to go and vouch for him or he would most certainly have been shot. I don't think he will risk doing that sort of thing in war time again. The next morning the great affair was providing the men with paper and envelopes to write to their families. They took the opportunity too to make their confessions. M. le Directeur was busy before Mass, after Mass, all the morning and towards 11 a soldier came to me, saluted and said that M. le Directeur wanted M. le Curé sent for to help as he couldn't get done. You can believe that I didn't need telling twice. In ten minutes our Curé and the one from Wignael were there to help, but in the afternoon it was the same and at 5 o'clock they were still there. One poor man had not managed to go and had to mount guard the following day until the troops were leaving. In despair he sent one of the sisters to enquire if M. le Directeur would not come to him as he could not leave his post. Needless to say he went. He must have been tired when he had finished but I do not expect he minded. As they had not received orders they spent a good part of the morning manoeuvring in the fields outside the convent. I was sent up to the museum with the children to watch. It was really very interesting but I pitied the poor men in the broiling heat with their heavy clothes and knapsacks especially as they had so carefully cleaned themselves from head to foot and the dust was frightful. It was rather distressing too to see them rushing through a field of uncut oats. Of course they may have to do it in a skirmish of any kind but it cannot improve the crops. They were here two nights and finally received orders to leave next morning. They left practically at a minute's notice half of them not having had the time to dine. The second night other troops had joined on and we certainly had over 1,000 men sleeping here. You should see our poor floors. I don't believe they will ever come clean again. They are simply filthy but it is quite useless to attempt to do anything as the same thing may happen again and again before the war is over. They left three sick men behind them who were to go to the hospital at Louvain and would be fetched we were told. So they were for next day. A Red Cross motor car arrived fitted up with mattresses and who do you think the chauffeur proved to be? Well he was the son of Monsieur de Broqueville, the War Minister, whose name you will see in the papers every day of your life just at present. He is the soldiers' hero and darling. One man was too ill to be moved so he is still here. There was one pouring wet day and he was out all the time and then had to sleep in a draughty barn, so took a chill which will almost certainly develop into consumption. He is longing to get to the war but is too weak even to stand properly. He is most anxious not to go to the hospital as there he is sure he could not have a shot at the enemy if they arrived. The men are most grateful for all that was done for them and some of the sick men made small offerings from their little all, one 50 centimes another 25 and so forth, because they said they had been so kindly looked after. They had been told that the Gs. [Germans] aimed chiefly at the officers at Liege so that in certain regiments hardly an officer was left alive, so we made black linen covers for their shakos [a tall military hat] and swords and gold stripes so that there was nothing bright and shiney to aim at or to distinguish them. I am so glad we did, for we were told yesterday that ours are the next to be sent to the front and really we all feel as sorry as if they were members of the family. Poor fellows, some of them have left their wives and children unprovided for. One called from this village was to have been married that very morning, another had been married just two days. There has been a good deal of fighting in the neighbourhood, but not very near; near enough to hear the cannon though, and I am certain that for a time they were afraid they would arrive in this direction. There are 60 men to guard the 3 bridges, ours and the two an hour's walk on either side. Campenhout and Wygmael. Our soldiers left on Thursday at midday and we were quite calm and peaceful again until 9 o'clock the next evening when 40 *gardes civiques* [civic guards, civilian soldiers] on horseback arrived. They were the *gardes civique* of Liege at least a part of it and had been to Louvain whence they had been sent here. Of course we have not stabling for 40 horses so they hunted about in the village at different farms and finally about 15 minus their horses came to sleep here. They stayed all day Saturday (the Assumption) and Sunday leaving finally at about 5 o'clock on Monday afternoon. Once more a little peace when late on Tuesday afternoon they told us that 250 soldiers were coming to lodge the night at the *externat*. Cavalry this time. Eventually it transformed itself into about 1,200. Never did I pass such a night. We did not know that more than 250 were coming until after 7 o'clock and they did not begin to arrive until past 10 o'clock; the very last got here at 2 a.m. So you can imagine. The farm yard and the big ones' playground were crowded with horses. It was midnight before the bulk of the men had found place and we had far more officers than the time before so that when the *petit pensionnat* [small boarding school] was full we had to go and make beds in all the *chambres à loger*, about 20 in one of the dormitories besides some sleeping in the infirmary and some on mattresses on the floor in the parlours. Every minute telegraphists arrived with messages for this or that officer and nobody knew who was sleeping where so that someone had to accompany them wherever there were officers sleeping to make enquiries. At last at 2.15 a.m. things seemed to be fairly calm and the *réveil* [reveille, wake up time] was announced for 5 o'clock so I went to bed. Barely had I gone 10 minutes when a motor dashed up with fresh orders and at half-past two those poor tired men had to be up again. By four there was not a soldier here except three sick men in the ambulance. It seemed there was trouble in the direction of Rothselaer [Rotsellar], Werchter and Aerschot [Aarschot], all villages within less than an hour's walk and alas it is only too true. Naturally everyone here in the village is terror-stricken and locking up to depart. In the afternoon refugees began to arrive from different places to ask for hospitality here, hoping that our Red Cross flags would protect then. Everyone who could put in any sort of claim to our consideration and many who have none seem to be here. Old pupils, relations of nuns, servants or villagers, the nuns from Wespelaer, etc., etc. We seem to be a regular city of refuge, and a none too safe one it seems to me. We spent all our time making beds in the dormitories which were filled as if by magic with these unfortunate people. During the afternoon four wounded soldiers were brought in, one in a dying condition with a bullet through him entering at the back about the hip somewhere and crossing his body coming out by the abdomen right on the other side. They had to give him the last sacraments at once but he is still alive this morning and there is just a wee shred of hope that we may save him. Poor fellow, he is so edifying and quite willing if need be to offer up his life for the welfare of the country and the cessation of this dreadful war. I cannot make out what the English are doing and why they don't come actively to the rescue of our gallant little troops.

August 20, 1914.

While I am writing to you now Aug. 20th there is regiment after regiment of G. soldiers marching in splendid order past the house. They seem unending as far as numbers are concerned and quite fresh. They have been going past now for quite three hours and do not appear likely to come to an end. How can our poor soldiers, tired out and more than decimated resist them if England and France do not do something more than admire their bravery and determination. All this last lot of men had been at Liege and related enough to fill pages.

August 23, 1914.

I shall not get much written even now after this long pause in my diary. I have perhaps 20 minutes at my disposal unless something unforeseen occurs which is generally the case at present, and the events since I last wrote would in themselves make a book of horrors. I told you the Gs. were passing—well, they have been passing on and off ever since. The first alarm came where I left off writing and made the dash up above. M. [Mère] Mathilde burst into the room saying she was afraid perhaps someone was at the window as there was a dreadful German down below who insisted on making the round of the house to see if we had no soldiers or arms hidden. I rushed off at once to the *moyennes* [middle school, grades 6–9, elementary to high school] to see that they were alright and crossing the *salle des fêtes* I saw some half dozen of them fully armed in the middle of those poor frightened villagers who had taken refuge here. They went all over the house everywhere absolutely even into the cloisters, cells, infirmary, cellars, etc., etc., had cupboards opened to be sure nothing was hidden in them and eventually went away declaring themselves satisfied but leaving a sick man apparently badly wounded in the throat.

September 4, 1914.

Excuse writing. I have a gathered finger [inflamed swelling at the tip of a finger]. So much has happened that I have quite lost count of time and the order in which they (the events) took place but I will endeavour to continue now for half an hour to the music of the cannon which is booming away somewhere close at Malines we think. Towards evening they arrived again and insisted upon setting a guard for the house. The two parlours by the door had to be emptied and mattresses placed. Then they insisted on making a second round of the house. Half the people had already gone to bed. The second section was full of poor folk with screaming babies trying to sleep on straw or mattresses and two dormitories of people of better class. They made all the men get up and assemble in the *salle des fêtes*. You never saw such a state of mind as we were all in. Nobody knew what was going to happen. I don't think they quite knew themselves but were frightened at seeing so many men and feared for themselves during the night. At first there was a talk of sending them all away to their respective dwellings but that of course was quite impractical, as many of them have no longer a roof to call their own and in any case they would have been killed or made prisoners on the way. Finally they decided to keep everyone (men of course) for the night in the *salle des fêtes* under guard. Two soldiers fully armed in the *salle* itself and three on the bridge. Every two hours the guard changed. You can imagine that nobody felt like going to bed, even the children were told to lie down fully dressed in case of alarm. One officer took off his boots, put on light shoes so that he could not be heard and thus equipped paraded the house wherever he felt inclined all night. Delightful wasn't it!!! Meanwhile our poor dying soldier had expired at midday, and one of the nuns at 5 p.m. to add to our other troubles. The German soldiers buried the soldier early next morning. They then departed but the march past continued. In the afternoon—oh I had forgotten to tell you two of the most appalling incidents of this first visit. They went to the presbytery, an officer and some men fully armed, knocked at the door and when nobody opened they broke it in. They found their way to the room where M. le Curé was with his sister, his servant and the Curé of Wygmael and stood over them with pistols cocked saying they had the right to kill them as it was the priests who excited the people against them. Finally they changed their tactics and insisted on his taking down the Belgian flag which was still floating in the church. Naturally it was not his doing, but was placed there by the *commune* [local administration] so they brought him here under guard to fetch the cleric who had the key of the tower and then the two had to go up with armed soldiers behind them to take down the flag. During the night the whole sky was lit up by the burning of the factory, La Corbeille at Wespelaer. They had found powder or ammunition of some sort there and burnt it down in revenge. The horrors committed at Wespelaer defy description and the poor Curé had aged 20 years when we last saw him bringing a poor cancerous woman whom they had shot (after killing her mother and brother) here to be looked after. The poor creature had been two days in a ditch unable to get help. The Gs. saw her but would do nothing and no one else dared to venture out of doors.

September 17, 1914.

So much has happened since I last wrote that I really hardly know myself. Everything is jumbled up in my memory. We really seem to be absolutely the centre of the German operations and have never been without German soldiers in the house since that first day. I am now writing in the ambulance where I am keeping watch until midnight and there are two sentinels outside the door in the little ones' playground. As every pane of glass is smashed they might just as well be inside as far as I am concerned. We have been so dreadfully busy in the ambulance that I have been quite unable to keep as I had intended a sort of diary for you. I did not even say office or anything for days together. I will try now to continue events in their chronological order but I am afraid I shall not succeed. The next day in the afternoon arrived a soldier to say that we had to lodge 60 officers, Germans of course. As there was no help for it we prepared a dormitory. They are all the same in one respect. They go about in abject terror of their lives knowing that they are in the enemy's country. The Burgomaster had made himself scarce so they took the poor Curé prisoner and he slept all night guarded by fully-armed soldiers and next morning said his Mass in between two soldiers for fear he escaped. He was held responsible for the whole village and was told that if anyone shot at a soldier he would be the first one shot. Poor man, he was in a state and it is no idle threat they make, for they have done frightful things pretending that civilians had shot at soldiers when they had done no such thing. One family here had their house burnt down because some B. [Belgian] soldiers had hidden behind it—which they had a perfect right to do—then a G. soldier fired on them in the garden. The father and a boy of 12 were both wounded in the shoulder, the mother had a bayonet wound on her face and the little girl of 7 was shot in the back of her leg high up so badly that in spite of all we could do she died after about a week. Those four we had here to take care of, but besides that two girls of 17 and 18 were killed as well as the baby of two which the mother was holding in her arms. The uncle lived next door and three or four of his sons were killed at the same time. Well, these gentlemen had a general—a very important one it appears—with them and required 2 *salles* one for writing, etc., and one for the council of war or something of the sort. It was their État Major [Army General Staff] (whatever that may be in English) I believe. During the night more illuminations and fireworks. Poor folks kept pouring in with bundles containing all they had been able to save, sent off by the Germans who immediately burnt down their houses. As I said before we already had a number of people here. Well the soldiers broke open the doors of the houses pillaged everything and destroyed what they could not carry away. They broke into the poor school and lodged there the night doing as much damage as they could. Unfortunately the straw which had been put there for our soldiers and the lamps were still there so they had a splendid time on the whole and opened cupboards carrying off or tearing all the clothes prepared for the prizes and left the place in a filthy mess which I will not attempt to describe to you in detail—it was too low. We have had such frequent repetitions of that kind of thing that I will not attempt to describe each one in detail—indeed I couldn't if I would.

I wonder if you got my P.C. [postcard]. A Dutch delegate, brother of one of our old pupils, passed here and offered to send letters for us by Holland but we thought letters too dangerous, they might compromise him or us and one cannot be too careful nowadays. I told you that the house had been badly damaged by cannon in a skirmish between the Bs. at Wespelaer and the Gs. on this side of the canal. They stay here always to keep the bridge as it is the road they use to go to Louvain, but it is very rare that we have the same troops more than a day or two. I think it was August 28 and then the wounded began to arrive. We already had 13 or 14 but by the next morning we had over 50 and some dreadful cases. They brought two dead Gs. and buried them right away in the garden, then they brought a man who had had his arm shot right off—awful it was—and another man shot through the lungs. In the afternoon we were giving extreme unction to a Pole shot through the head when they announced 7 Belgians badly wounded, poor fellows they were in such a state that we gave them the last sacraments as they arrived with the least possible ceremony for fear they did not live till the end. Of the 7 we only succeeded in saving one—two died that same evening. You can believe that we were pretty busy in the ambulance after that. Several died of course, but many began to get convalescent when an extra objectionable lot of men arrived apparently commanded by an army doctor. He was terrified for his life and tried to hide it by a great deal of bluster. He stationed sentinels all over the house and nobody might move from where they were while he once more searched the house from attic to cellar. I had just slipped out of the ambulance into the garden to try to say Vespers and get a little fresh air at the same time. When I came back I found a sentinel (in front of the door) who refused to let me enter. I thought the wisest thing to do was to pretend I didn't understand though his gestures were significant enough. I was laughing and trying to explain in my German that I absolutely must go to my sick—he trying to be polite and do his duty at the same time though he felt it was idiotic and showed it when one of the convalescent Germans who knew me perfectly by sight came along and I called him to the rescue. Naturally he could do nothing but try to explain what I wouldn't understand and finally he passed though saying to his comrade "I can pass anyhow". "Of course" laughed the other which I pretended to understand as meant for me and slipped through at the same time the sentinel conveniently turning his back and pretending not to see. I don't mind admitting now that my heart went pit-a-pat in spite of my laughing exterior and I did not feel at all sure that I should not get a bullet in my back or something of the kind. The search was made for ages, cupboards, boxes, etc., had to be opened and it was 8 o'clock instead of 6 when we were eventually able to think of supper. Next day he packed off all the Germans and Poles (pupils) and took with him as prisoners 23 of our convalescent Belgian soldiers—oh we did feel sick, but what could we do! We shan't forget his passage here in a hurry. He insisted on sleeping in the ambulance with two others as he was a doctor but stipulated absolutely that the door of the corridor should be locked and nobody but nuns be allowed to pass during the night. Of course in the ambulance we are always two at least during the night and more when necessary and just then we had several critical cases. We had a *vicaire* [assistant priest in a parish] from some parish in Antwerp who got stranded here with two Seminarists trying to walk back from Louvain for trains and posts are quite things of the past so far as we are concerned. He, the priest, acts as chaplain in the ambulance and has proved invaluable for nights together he slept on a mattress on the ground ready for sick calls and we insisted that he had to be there that night too as it was absolutely necessary. Finally we obtained that much. The day after that man left the ambulance from Brussels sent 3 motors to fetch some of our men and we sent 16 I think so that our numbers were considerably diminished and eventually we were left with only 7 very badly wounded.

After that arrived a lot of sailors they were here quite a long time—a week I should think—because of the Naval Victory of the English at Heligoland. We knew no details but they said there was nothing for them to do at sea just then which was a good sign and they hate the English so whole-heartedly that that is another good sign. They had with them 2 doctors. The principal was a particularly nice man. He brought with him 4 Belgian prisoners badly wounded and 2 Germans and tended them like a father. On the Friday we heard the cannon quite close all day long. It was at Werchter and Wackerzeel and no end of damage was done. Several wounded were brought in amongst others 3 or 4 officers who were put in a room apart. Next morning at about 4 began our turn. I never wish to live through the like again. The Germans had taken their stand behind the farm buildings so far as I can make out and the Belgians must have known that they had had their headquarters here. In any case they made our convent the aim of their cannon balls with dire results. The whole community spent the day in the cellars with a few exceptions. I remained in the ambulance with two others and I can assure you I never wish to spend another such day. As far as I can make out, the object of the affair was to bring down the belvedere as we call it—that little watch tower by the big reservoir.

September 20, 1914.

As I said before the Germans seem to have made us their head-quarters and a woman from the Wackerzeel said that a Belgian officer had been stationed in the church tower there watching what went on with field glasses—that he could see the G. Officers going in and out quite distinctly and kept repeating "Have an eye on the convent". However that may be they certainly had their cannon mouths on the convent and from 4 a.m. to midday it was simply terrible in the ambulance. I fully expected every moment to be my last at least I ought to have done but somehow I couldn't believe that any real harm would come to us after all the prayers that are offered up daily here. By midday there was hardly a pane of glass intact in the whole of the new wing, the walls are perforated like cardboard in places one "*obus*" [artillery shell] (I really don't know the term in English; it can't be cannon ball for they are not balls at all but shaped so[4] and filled with little bullets about the size of a marble which scatter when they burst and do no end of damage) rolled the whole length of the corridor after passing through the two doors, another along the *moyennes* playground and we were in a room between the two. Bricks and glass were falling right and left. Our beautiful convent is a sight to behold. Up in the *moyennes* dormitory a pipe was pierced so that there was an inundation which went down three stories and now we have no water in that part of the house and no electricity. Further there are no workmen to be had so that the damage cannot be repaired. In the afternoon the cannon banged away on the other side of the house so that in the ambulance it was not quite so terrible though bad enough, and the wounded began to arrive so that I was kept pretty busy and had less time to realise the awful situation than in the morning. It went on until dark and as soon as it stopped the wounded and dying

4. Here Mother Marie Georgine drew a rough sketch of a projectile or can-non shell to illustrate her point.

poured in. It was a dreadful sight. We had our own doctor on the premises. He has been here ever since the war began and we had besides two German naval doctors who had come here with the sailors and the elder of whom is a particularly nice man. I worked with him and two Red Cross men from about five o'clock till after 10 p.m. binding up legs, arms, heads, etc., and the other two doctors were doing the same in other rooms. Everywhere was packed and improvised stretchers all along both sides of the corridor. By evening we had over 250 wounded here. The *Salle Ste. Marie* was covered with straw and the disabled slept there while here in the ambulance there was hardly room to move. We did have a time. In one room I had 10 officers to look after and in another 12 soldiers of whom 3 died. The others of course had quite as much if not more but we were all so busy we had no time to bother about anything but our own immediate work. Tired as I was I did not go to bed before I had said a Te Deum in thanksgiving for mercies received. Not a single life lost in spite of a whole day's bombarding. There was one dead soldier whom we could not get buried on account of the battle, he had died that very morning, so we had placed him in a little room at the end of the corridor by the lift— removing the parrot to do so. He had the cupboards and the three doors of the place on the top of him so that had he been alive he must most certainly have been killed and the parrot placed just outside to make room for him was unhurt. Next day Sunday the same thing took place at Haecht. We could hear it all day long. Having such a small house it was of course much worse for the poor sisters there who had already had a dreadful time. They had been taken in a body prisoners to Louvain, a week or two ago because they were unable to produce one of the doctors who was working in their ambulance. He had been sent for to attend someone in the village and during his absence the Germans came to enquire. Naturally he was not forthcoming and never did come to light as apparently he also was taken prisoner en route. The poor sisters were marched to Louvain between two lines of soldiers and lodged in some filthy room in the barracks or hospital, I forget which. They were practically starved as provisions were not forthcoming and eventually some went to German Ursulines and others returned to Haecht only to get this second affair. As far as we can understand they were in the cellars until 10 o'clock at night with the house falling about their ears and then were sent off to Louvain with 46 wounded under an escort of German soldiers. Two of the soldiers who helped them as far as Louvain were here the other day, one of them a nice Catholic boy told us about it with tears in his eyes. Since then some of our sisters have been under escort several times to see what they could save. They say it is quite heart-rending to see the state of the house. The chapel is an absolute ruin. Nothing remained standing except just the tabernacle and three statues. No priest was allowed to accompany to bring back the Blessed Sacrament so the nuns had to do it and they had to get one of the soldiers to break open the door of the tabernacle. The man was a Catholic and worked away at the lock for over an hour hoping to be able to force it but could not—when he found that he really had to hack down the door he cried like a child they say, and was only consoled when he himself rescued the Blessed Sacrament. He used to be an altar boy as a child and is cherishing the hope of relating to his parish-priest how he himself had the monstrance and ciborium in his hands. He was a perfect Godsend to the nuns and helped them tremendously. They saved several cart loads of linen, eatables, medicines, etc., besides altar vessels and vestments but of course there are quantities of things that cannot be saved and the building itself is in a dreadful state. The village church too is razed to the ground. At Wespelaer they are stabling the horses in the church as they have done nearly everywhere round here. There is scarcely a village anywhere within an hour and a half from here where there has not been fighting and sometimes several times. Most of the villages are burnt or partially and the willful destruction is frightful besides cruelty. Of course one cannot generalize for individual cases but I have heard so many terrible stories from people to whom they have happened or who have seen the things with their own eyes that I really begin to think that they are nearly all barbarians. They do such dreadful things and all the time are such cowards. While we were being bombarded I went into one of the rooms where there were already a few German soldiers *hors de combat* [out of military action due to injury, wounded, disabled]. As we had not enough bedsteads they slept on two mattresses placed on the floor. I wanted to see how many wounded could still be placed there and if the beds were in order. I found four mattresses pell mell and took hold of one to arrange the four mattresses into two beds when, to my astonishment found a soldier underneath. The wretched man was not ill at all except with fright, and was lying in between his two mattresses for safety. Several were brought in with sunstroke? or syncope? a polite way of expressing excess of fear. Poor men—many of them have no more the vocation of a soldier than I have and only march because they can't help themselves. Two or three of the men who died here were the fathers of 6 children and we had about 16 deaths in three days besides those who never reached us alive. No end were drowned in the canal. Some are said to have drowned themselves from fear but I doubt if that is true but certainly over 30 of the sailors were shot by the Belgian soldiers as they tried to swim across. There is no means of getting to know how many were killed for the Germans will not own up to how great their loss was and it must have been very great from things they let drop and besides they were without artillery. They only received cannons the next day in time for poor Haecht. The nice doctor I told you about came back to see us yesterday, and he had received the iron cross for his conduct during the battle here. He was very proud of it and said it was the highest decoration in Germany and only given in time of war. I suppose it corresponds with our Victoria Cross. He was packed off with his sailors almost immediately after the battle to make room for a troop of soldiers who arrived with 300 Red Cross men and 9 doctors. We say he was sent away because he showed his sympathy for us too openly. The motor ambulances have been coming daily from Brussels to fetch the wounded so that we are gradually getting emptied. Tonight we have only 5 Belgians and 12 Germans left in the ambulance and we expect some of those to be fetched tomorrow. We still remain their centre for the disabled and have about 50 men in the *Salle Ste. Marie* either tired out with forced marches or slightly wounded but so far I have not had much to do with that quarter. I have been quite busy enough in the ambulance itself and have learnt quite a lot about bullet-wounds, etc. Now the weather has changed and we have had wind and rain for the last few days. That has set in a new fashion and it is colds, bronchitis and pneumonia that have begun. It is too dreadful to think of if that is to continue all the winter and here the house is nothing but draughts with the broken windows and we shall most certainly be unable to heat even if we have sufficient coal, which I doubt as several of the hot water pipes are damaged. These men who are here now are not half as nice as the sailors. Of the 9 doctors only one is nice and a few of the Red Cross men. They have two chaplains with them, a Catholic and a Lutheran. The Catholic one said a military Mass here on Friday morning served by two soldiers and about 50 of the men came to it and sang for themselves. This morning there were about 20 at the 9 o'clock Mass. Until now we have always managed to keep the watch tower closed against them. I feel sure it was for fear that they made use of it that the Belgians bombarded it, it hadn't been used though for you can understand that we do not feel any desire to help them. Now, however, they have obliged us to let them go up and they keep watch all night replacing each other every two hours. It does make me feel sick at heart, yet one is perfectly helpless and can do nothing. The might is in their hands at present but I cannot think that it will be long before they are crushed as they deserve. My blood simply boils when I think of all the atrocities they have committed in this neighborhood.

September 28, 1914.

We have done quite a lot towards saving in various villages this last week as we got passes from the Commander to save in our various convents and bring what we could here. I went with one of the nuns to our poor school at Delle. That was all right so was the church comparatively and we were able to save the vestments, etc., but the Curé's house had been ransacked from attic to cellar and all the drawers and cupboards opened and their contents emptied on to the floor. You never saw such a mess—naturally the linen, etc., had disappeared and many other things. However, that was better than the rest of the village where hardly a house remained standing, nothing but the blackened skeletons of walls. From there we went to Bucken to save the Blessed Sacrament. The Church had been completely burned as well as the village and a monk who helped the Curé had just managed to hide the Blessed Sacrament in an oven of a house already burnt when he and the Curé were taken prisoners. They were brutally treated, kicked and battered about with the but-end of guns, etc. There is not a priest anywhere in the neighbourhood except our three. All have been taken and treated abominably. We do not know for certain what has happened to most of them. Some are going about dressed as civilians, others are supposed to have escaped to England. Let's hope that it is true. The servant knew where the Sacrament was hidden and went with us to show us the way. The ciborium was in a tin biscuit box right inside a stove in the midst of ruins. There is hardly a house left standing in all the village. You never saw such ruin and desolation. There is absolutely nothing left to save—everything is burnt. We brought back the Blessed Sacrament ourselves for want of a priest, a memorable incident of which I shall boast to the end of my days. We made friends with the Catholic chaplain of the troops and he went to save the Blessed Sacrament at Wespelaer and at Wygmael besides which we saved the altar vessels, vestments, etc. I went down to Wespelaer twice and there you see the same scenes of desolation only besides the houses being burnt they have huge holes in the walls made by the cannons. We brought up car loads of things. The Curé had promised to go to the village church at Haecht and St. Adrian for the Blessed Sacrament but their troops were ordered off suddenly to make way once more for the famous État Major with its *Exzellenz* [high ranking officials] and Generals, staff officers, etc. They have taken up their abode here since yesterday and are far worse than anything we have had here so far, worse than they were themselves last time. They have some Austrian soldiers with them only officers here though. The house is a regular barracks. They walk about choosing their own rooms and marking their names on the doors with chalk. The children's kitchen is for the preparation of the officers' mess and has a soldier cook with half a dozen aids. Every class and dormitory is occupied, every *salle* in use, it requires all our ingenuity to protect the cloisters from their invasion. The officers managed to consume over 70 bottles of wine yesterday. I have no doubt they will do even better to-day. Barrels of beer disappear too with coffee to drown the lot while the simple soldiers complain that they have barely dry bread. May they revolt! I desire nothing so heartily. The very sight of the German troops makes me feel sick and our danger is very great. The fighting continues all round us, we can always hear the cannon booming away. We may have a second edition of September 12th any time. Tomorrow they are trying to send the children who remain as far as Brussels and thence to Holland in the hope of getting them eventually to their various destinations. England should present little difficulty once they are in Holland but for the Russian Poles it is another matter. Mère Antoine and Mère Xaveria who have arrived from India on a begging expedition after an absence of 12 years, got here just as the war became serious. They saw the first real signs of it at Aden. As they are wasting their time (from a missionary point of view) here they are going with the children to England to perfect their English and I am going to try to send this [letter] by them. If you get it and wish for more first hand news of our adventures here you had better visit them. They will almost certainly be at one of the two houses where you visited me and by writing to one you could find out at which. The fact of your receiving this would be a sign that they have arrived safe and sound. They would be able to tell you many things that I can hardly write. I should so dearly love to know what has become of you all and of the 5 who were in Germany but there seems to be no means. Very best love to those whom this reaches!! Pray for us all for we need it badly and the poor homeless folks by whom we are surrounded. I will stop now in hope of getting this off.

October 18, 1914.

The other letter hasn't gone yet after all, but I am making a fresh start, as I finished that up hoping to send it by M. Antoine. They had hoped to send the few English children we still have here back home by the same opportunity, but it never came. Eventually M. Antoine and M. Xaveria went off to Louvain by themselves hoping from there to be able to make their way to Holland and eventually to England. We have not heard from them since so conclude they have been successful, and now there is a talk of Mère A. also risking it with the children. It is a dreadful responsibility having them in such risky times, and though things are comparatively quiet here for the last week, there is no saying how long they will remain so, and in any case it will be as much as we can do to tide over the winter so that the less mouths there are to feed the better. The ruthless waste and destruction is terrible when you think of the misery and want that must necessarily be the result. I have asked Mère A. if she does reach England to let you know, so that she can give you news of us and you can let me know through her how you and Mabel are and if you have had any news of the other five about whom I feel very anxious.

This morning I have once more written you two postcards in the hope that one at least will reach you. I have already sent you a letter early in August and a postcard on two different occasions by a Dutchman brother of an old pupil who is travelling about and undertook to send them safely by Holland. I take it that you got nothing, as this morning we received several letters through the Dutch Embassy at Louvain, and amongst them a card from the Convent at Eisder enquiring about us in general, and saying that they had received enquiries from my family about me. I immediately wrote you another card by the Embassy and trust it will reach you; if only I could get something from you how glad I should be.

I think that I must have told you that the German État Major came back. They sent on an officer to demand 60 bedrooms; naturally we said that we did not possess them being a boarding school and not an hotel. However, he returned two days later saying that we had no choice about the matter but had to take them in whether we liked it or no. As we had not sufficient separate rooms, a number of the officers would sleep in the dormitories but must have two *chambrettes* [alcoves] apiece. On the Sunday they arrived and they stayed for a fortnight leaving once more on a Sunday. The kitchen where the children learn cooking was used as the Officers' kitchen, and their own cook with several assistants prepared the meals, which seemed to go on all day long. The big ones' refectory served for the officers' mess. Breakfast à *la fourchette* ["breakfast with forks," a large breakfast] from 5–9 a.m. lunch at 12 or any other time for single individuals, tea, or rather coffee on the same principle; then at 7 p.m. a huge dinner. The refectory [dining hall] was never empty before 10.30 p.m. all the time they were here, and it was usually after midnight. They hinted to Rev. Mother Gen. that they would like us to wait on them, but she managed to get out of it somehow, pleading that we were already tired out with sick nursing, etc., so the orderlies waited at table, but every night two sisters had to stay up to look after the cooks, two to arrange the ref. [refectory] after they had finished, and two to answer the door, for there were constant alerts. When they condescended to go to bed (any time between 11 a.m. and 2 p.m.) [11 p.m. and 2 a.m.?] the four first could go too as soon as the breakfast table was prepared for next morning, but the two at the door had to be replaced at midnight by two others, as it could never be left alone. The amount they managed to eat, drink and smoke passes all comprehension. They drank several hundred bottles of wine while they were here, and after they had destroyed Malines their provision motor car used to make daily visits there to pillage, and then they drank champagne like water. Not a night passed that several of them were not drunk, they used to stagger to their rooms and often didn't know the way. The orderlies followed the example of their masters, often drinking out of the bottle on their way to the ref. and also being careful to remove the bottles when they were still half full. Besides that they made a point of stealing as many as possible in spite of the fact that they were kept under lock and key, and the place changed to prevent them. I really don't blame them seeing that their masters did worse. There were two Excellences, I don't know how many Generals and 60 or 70 other officers, almost all noblemen according to their own showing, but indeed a Sunday school child could have given them a lesson in cleanliness or table manners. Our tinies would not make the tablecloth in the state they made it in a day if we left it on the table a fortnight. The principal was the Excellency Von Beseler [General Hans Hartwig von Beseler], who was charged with the taking of Antwerp, and all the time they were here there was talk of Antwerp and how long it would take, etc., etc. All the men that were here seemed very previous and kept well out of danger, but there was a lot of going to and fro. There were always about a dozen motor cars—often more—in front of the house ready to fly off at a moment's notice. The telephone was established in the piano rooms and wireless telegraphy in the *salle de coupe* [fitting room]. All the big ones' classes nearly were *bureaux* [offices] for some general or other with huge placards on the door indicating what department was established there. The *salle des fêtes* was a printing place and a depôt for maps. I took lessons in lithography from a Catholic soldier who made himself very amiable. He told me afterwards that his cousin was an Ursuline at Cologne, so that accounted for the attraction. The officer in charge there gave me and the two nuns who were with me some splendid maps. A huge one of Belgium and half of France with every village marked, and 7 detailed ones of different parts of Belgium marking every road and field. He gave us each a copy of the 8 maps, so I think we did well. The first section served as a sitting room for the Excellency and his staff; the second section for other personages, so that we literally could not call the house our own.

October 24, 1914.

On the Friday, October 9th, there was a great deal of excitement towards midday. The soldiers went about announcing with beaming faces that Antwerp had fallen. When I told my printer that I didn't believe it, he said that the Burgomaster of Antwerp with a Sheriff and two other civilians were at that minute with the officers in the second section arranging the conditions of the capitulation. "If you don't believe me", he added, "you have only to walk across the bridge and you will see them through the window". Needless to say I did, and it was only too true, so you see this house will be quite historical after the war. The four of them lunched with the officers, but apparently there was very little talk, and almost immediately after they went away without anyone having been able to say a word to them. You can imagine how sad we all felt. Several officers went off to Antwerp they said, but all the same there was not the excitement or enthusiasm that such an event ought to have produced. That evening happened to be one of my nights to watch till midnight. Just after 8 o'clock they arrived with a General and another officer whom they said they had taken in one of the forts at Antwerp. They were hugely delighted with their capture, and put the two into the old pupils' refectory with a sentinel posted in front of both doors and (as we afterwards discovered) they stopped the keyhole of the door of one of the piano rooms with a gun cartridge, because the window opened into the refectory. I suppose it was an extra precaution to prevent us having any communication with them. That pokey little room was intended to serve the couple of them as dining and bedroom. You can imagine how we felt at one of our Generals being treated with so little consideration. Protest after protest was raised, but nothing was to be obtained. One officer went so far as to say that it was more than good enough—a cellar would be too good for a Belgian General—low, wasn't it? But I think he must have been over-excited to forget himself so far—however, he paid for it dearly. Mère Ambroisine was there and let out the vials of her wrath upon him saying that it was low and vulgar to treat people of distinction like that, and that if he did not know what was due to them we did! The end of it was that they were really ashamed I think, and probably afraid of it coming out later on to add to the bad name they have already made for themselves, and they tried to patch the matter up by allowing us to make up beds for them in S. Joseph and St. Angele, and two parlours, one of which you people generally occupy when you are here. St. Angele is the one I first saw Daddy in, and S. Joseph is where Dora generally sits and where you have your meals when you are alone. They had their supper in the old pupils' refectory and were treated like the German officers for very shame's sake, even receiving a bottle of champagne, and they slept in the rooms prepared for them with a sentinel in front of each door all night. Next morning there was a great talk of the Excellency, Von Beseler, being decorated for the taking of Antwerp, though he really didn't appear to have done much, seeing that the town capitulated, so that it should not be completely bombarded and destroyed like so many others. It seems that Prince Waldemar, nephew of the Kaiser, the son of his brother Henry, was to come here on purpose and great preparations were made. A bedstead was put into the S. Joseph parlour and it was transformed into a proper bedroom to receive him. Well, evening came and he had not turned up and then once more very late some officers arrived with fresh captures. Another General—the Commander of Antwerp this time—and two officers. Imagine our delight to lodge the Belgian General in the bed they had prepared with such care for Prince Waldemar! This time the lesson had been learnt and there was not talk of cellars. All the same they behaved very badly, for they took the poor Commandant away next morning and paraded him in a motor car all round Brussels and then round Louvain—horrid wasn't it? However, those 5 officers and 40 soldiers seem to have been all that they got out of Antwerp—not so very glorious considering that they had expected to capture the town and the entire Army with it. In Germany they seem to have thought likewise. The lot of them left here on Sunday, the very least leaving in the small hours of Monday morning. Well it seems the same day Von Beseler committed suicide—this item of gossip of course, as I have seen no one who actually saw it or was present at the funeral if there was one, but I think it must be true, as I have heard it from so many different sides. Prince Waldemar did pass here in his motor, and the General went out to him, but he did not come in because I suppose he had no decoration to give. The story goes (but I won't vouch for it) that when Von Beseler arrived at Brussels, he received orders to return to Germany (or the other version has it to present himself before a

Council of War). He knew that the Kaiser was dissatisfied that he had required so much time to take Antwerp and was probably less satisfied still at the way it was ultimately taken, and fearing to be disgraced or shot preferred to shoot himself. Awful it seems to me, but the Governor of Louvain did the same thing (the German Governor I mean) and several other officers, so I suppose they think it better than to incur the Kaiser's anger even when it is no fault of theirs. It gives me the shivers when I think of it. Since then we are rid of the Germans at Thildonck [Tildonk] and have spent most of our time trying to clean up after them. While they were here, they were, amongst other things, trying to take the forts of Waelhem and Lierre, which put several of our convents in great danger of being bombarded. Rev. Mother General heard that Wavre Notre Dame and Lierre had both been burnt and consequently was very anxious to find out for herself to what extent it was true, and if anything could be done to help the nuns. She spoke to some officer about it, who assured her that nothing could be easier. They would arrange for her to go with Rev. Mother in one of the motors with some of the officers and they would be able to visit both convents and arrange what they liked, etc., etc. Accordingly full of faith they set off at 4.15 p.m. That last item alone would have been enough for me. They were taken a most roundabout way and when they protested that the correct way was . . . they were told that this was the way they—the Germans—always went, meaning, I suppose, the only safe route for them. Eventually they were brought without touching Wavre beyond it at a place between it and Lierre, but in sight of neither, and were planted there alone in the motor car with bullets whistling over their heads in all directions while the officers went to interview some General. They consoled them with the assurance that they were really in no danger, as all the bullets were directed at the forts much further afield on either side so would go over their heads. I do not think I should have felt precisely comfortable or reassured myself. In the end the officers returned, pointed out a great fire in the distance, and said that it was Lierre in flames, and consequently out of the question. They told them too that it was true about Wavre, that it was entirely burnt except the new church and a few piano rooms, but that they could not go there, and so they brought them back after all those emotions with nothing done at all. However, when we were free, two of the nuns set off on foot and arrived there safely to see for themselves. I don't know if you know the convent of Wavre Notre Dame by reputation. It is a foundation from here, of course, but quite independent. It is larger, more important, and more beautiful than this from all accounts. They had just built a fine church in Norman style a few years back and have a very flourishing normal school besides the boarding school. Many of our sisters have been there to study for their diplomas. Well, they had an ambulance like we did, but being surrounded by Belgians instead of Germans as we were, their Red Cross flag was really respected, and they had to lodge no soldiers, only to provide food which was fetched. They are situated on a hill, very exposed, and suffered greatly from the bombarding of the fort of Waelher, receiving the "*obus*" from both sides. Finally all the sisters left except 13, who had to stay for the ambulance, 11 of them being Germans. Eventually the house took fire (in several places I believe) and the German nuns got the German soldiers who were by that time on the scene to help them to escape. They had an awful time fleeing with the soldiers with bullets whizzing round them. But all the same they eventually got away and reached Germany safely. The two Belgians, however, would not stop there because they hoped they might still be able to do something to save at least part of their convent, and managed somehow to get back to Belgium by way of Holland. They had just arrived when our two nuns came to the rescue. They were quite young sisters almost afraid of their own undertaking lest they should be exposing themselves unnecessarily and unauthorized, for they could get no news of the other nuns who had left before them. That is one of the worst features of this awful war—no means of getting news. To be sure that they were doing the right thing they first went to Antwerp and found the Cardinal [Mercier], who said that they were doing quite right and that it was their duty to their community. What they found exceeded all description. There is absolutely nothing saved except the church, badly injured by a bomb, and a few of the pianos there had already been stolen and soldiers were there with a wagon to fetch more when they arrived and protested, finally gaining their point. The destruction is so complete that it seems hardly possible that all can be the result of accident. Even the things put in the cellars for safety are gone and the cellars apparently burnt separately, though there are no ashes or anything to account for the things that were in them. Our nuns found them utterly destitute with nothing but the clothes they had on them, and a few mattresses found under the church where the ambulance had been— the blankets had all been stolen. There was nothing else at all except coal in some cellars, which I suppose had been overlooked in the general pillage which had evidently taken place. When our two sisters came back with that news, you can image that help in the shape of food, clothing and bedding was sent off post haste by our superiors, who have been the providence of the unfortunate for miles round. I really do believe that we owe our happy and almost miraculous escape to their charity. Lierre it seems is also burnt, and Londerzeel too utterly and entirely, but so far no one has been there, at least to Lierre. The sisters from Wolvertem visited Londerzeel and came to report. Only the poor school remains intact, and that is a considerable distance from the convent.

November 3, 1914.

From Lierre the family of one of our sisters came and told us that everything except the Ecole Professional is destroyed, and that once more was apart from the convent. At Wilryck the nuns were sent away, and have now returned to find the building intact but completely pillaged. The nuns of Puers were also sent away by the Belgian soldiers because they were too exposed in the forts and they have taken refuge in England at West Malvern. We have now sent four sisters to take charge of the building, one of them is sister to the Superior. They arrived just in time, for people had arrived and were beginning to help themselves when the nuns put in an appearance, so that there all is more or less saved. No doubt many other of our convents have suffered too, but it is impossible to get certain news of those farther afield. Believe none of the rubbish you may hear about us. Not a soul in the house has been killed or even wounded, though such a thing is little short of miraculous. They house is badly bombarded but still quite habitable, and we have everything to be grateful for, so have the villagers whom we were able to save almost entirely, though, of course, we have had some terribly sad cases. One of our workmen was shot on his way here, and not being quite killed, was trampled to death and buried where he lay. At Werchter a poor woman protested against her husband being taken prisoner saying she had nine children to support. They immediately killed five and then enquired if she had still too many. I could give you dozens of other examples, but now there seems to be a certain opportunity of dispatching this, so I had better close for the moment. We have opened the poor schools again this week, as there is peace once more in our neighbourhood for the time being. May it continue for long!

November 17, 1914.

I am hoping against hope to get some news of you all eventually, but it is a long wait the more so that we have so little certain news and are constantly hearing contradictory rumours. You at least have newspapers more or less correctly informed and *free* but we have practically none and such as we get on rare occasions are obviously under German control. Since the departure of the État Major we have been comparatively quiet. We have done our very best to clean the house, but I do not believe it will ever be quite itself again. At present we have just one tenth of our children, i.e., thirty odd instead of three hundred odd, and we scarcely hope for more until the War is over. It stands to reason that people in other countries will not send their children over here at present and Belgian parents are afraid to be separated from their children less they should not meet again. True, things are quiet here now but there is no certainty that they will remain so and there is an uneasy feeling everywhere that the troops will pass again on their return journey even more violent and barbarous than when they came, though I doubt if it is possible. Meanwhile, we spend most of our time making clothes for the poor, for the suffering this Winter will be terrible. I went to Herent to-day. It is an hour from here and ½ an hour from Louvain. The whole length of the high road Louvain Malines from Herent to Bruken (a distance of over an hour) there is hardly a single house that is not entirely burnt and many houses not on the high road at all have been burnt as well. The result is that several families are trying charitably to live together in one house barely big enough for the owner and the guests are all people who possess absolutely nothing but the clothes they had on when they succeeded in escaping in August or September. Their houses were fired about their heads at Bruken and soldiers shot at them as they tried to escape. The church which the Curé had just spent several hundreds of pounds on restoring (out of his own private fortune) is completely burnt down and he and the Père Conventuel [a member of The Order of St. Francis] who helped him were taken prisoners and treated much as Chinese are accustomed to treat Xians. There is a convent [male community] of Conventuels at Louvain. They are very poor and one of the many branches of Franciscans. Some of their priests help the Curés in villages where there is no Vicaire going from Saturday to Monday. They hear confessions, etc., on Saturday, help all day Sunday and return to their convent on Monday. At Bruken there was one, venerable looking man with a long beard, middle aged, I should say. Unfortunately he and M. le Curé were both there and the Germans arrived and were taken prisoners. They were shamefully ill-treated, kicked, knocked about with the butt end of guns, etc., etc. until they were so bruised and stiff that they could barely drag themselves along. They were taken away with the other men, the Curé so ill that he had to walk with 2 sticks, which the soldiers amused themselves by knocking down for the pleasure of seeing him fall. At one place a soldier forced his mouth open and put his flask to it obliging him to drink saying that he would find it a little different to wine. The men who were there say it was urine!! They were all kept for three hours on their knees in front of a stake where already 2 men were lying out right open and naturally everyone thought his turn was coming next; eventually however the other prisoners were released but nobody knew what became of the two priests. Now in digging up the bodies they have been found. The Père was found with his eyes burnt out and the Curé was found in a grave with 4 or 5 civilians—he was stripped entirely and nose and ears cut off. They were only able to recognize him for certain by the boots which were underneath him and which his servant recognized at once. Dreadful isn't it? (The Curé of Herent was found with the carcass of a horse buried on the top of him). He was last seen alive by a lady who had herself been a prisoner but released and he had been then shot in the head. I do not know what further they may have done to him before finishing him off. He was taken as hostage for Herent having insisted that the Burgomaster (cousin of one of our nuns) should escape because of the way they had treated the Burgomaster of Aerschot, shooting him and his son in presence of his wife and other children.

November 24, 1914.

Yesterday we received news for one of the lay sisters that her two brothers, a brother-in-law, a sister-in-law, two children in one family, one a baby of a few days old and one child in another had all been killed during the passage of the troops at Tamines in Hainault. It seems that the people had taken refuge in the Church and the soldiers made the men come out shooting them all after which they committed further horrors. In all about 6[oo]to 700 people were killed. The women and young girls were stripped and then made to march in between the troops. The Curé was crucified against a wall and when he complained of thirst they amused themselves by shooting him down the middle so that he had a row of bullet holes like buttons down the middle of his body. They seem to have a fiendish delight in crucifying people especially priests. A woman was here the other day who saw one crucified near Namur and one of the Haecht nuns who was taken prisoner also saw the body of a priest who has evidently been crucified from the holes in hands and feet. I was told the other day that they had crucified children against doors and walls at Charleroi, but that I cannot vouch for. They had pierced the hands of the Curé of Bueken, but do not seem to have crucified him. Perhaps he expired before they had time to do more. From all accounts they played pitch and toss with his body flinging it in and out of the cart as they went along, but it is impossible to know all the details of the treatment he was subjected to. At the beginning of the War one of our workmen was shot on his way here and as they say he was not yet dead from his movements, they trampled on him with their great boots and then buried him (still alive) where he lay. They did the same to a young girl at Wespelaer and burnt the house over the head of an old man and his daughter. Half the horrors they have committed will never be known even after the War, for people are buried all over the place and half the time it is not known who they are and where they come from. At Herent there were quite 50 new graves all civilians, many of them women, several killed at the point of the bayonet. There is not a churchyard in the neighbourhood without its contingent and they say that things are infinitely worse in the two Flanders. The other day they came to dig up the body of one of the soldiers who died here. He was a medical student and his family who seemed to be quite nice people could not bear to have him buried as all were merely wrapped in a sheet or an old blanket. They sent a magnificent coffin to have him properly buried, and they wish to transfer his remains to the family vault when the war is over. Well there was some error in the names put on the tombs, and when they dug up where he was supposed to be they found a coffin; the next Soldier's!!! grave proved to contain a civilian dressed in corderoys and wrapped up in a tablecloth. Nobody seems to know anything about this individual, and I can only suppose that the German soldiers profited at the time when they were told off to bury our soldiers [and] to bury another of those they had murdered. Finally the fourth grave proved to contain a soldier's body, and I was sent for to identify him, as I had looked after him for the few hours he lived and prepared him for burial. Considering that he had been buried for nearly three months without a coffin, he was wonderfully preserved and not at all the fearsome sight I had anticipated.

December 13, 1914.

I got your letters safe from Holland the day before yesterday and was so delighted that I nearly embraced Rev. Mother. How glad I am that Dora, Ethel and Gladys are safe home again. It is hardly to be wondered at that you could get no news of us for a time. The Germans were so precious afraid of their lives that they would let nobody come near while they were here. M. Antoine on her travels met a gentleman who told her that he had come with another (both Red Cross) to see if we were in danger and to take away any who wished to leave; but when they had got as far as the Cygne the Germans took them, tore off their armlets and shut them up in the cellar of the hotel whence they managed to escape a few days after. Then again there was a man amongst the Red Cross men who came to dig up the soldier I told you of, who related that he also had been sent from Louvain with an automobile to fetch the children. (We had asked the Dutch Representative, and I suppose he had been to the American Consul). At any rate the motor was not allowed to pass, and had to go back again. So you see we were a great deal too well protected when we didn't want to be. Perhaps we shall still hear of other attempts that were made. Naturally, we knew absolutely nothing of them at the time.

I think I did tell you that M. le Directeur of Haecht had been taken prisoner with several other priests. For weeks and weeks we could get no news whatever and concluded that he had been murdered like so many others. They say it is 180 for this diocese alone, but I do not know if that is correct. I only know personally of the three in the immediate neighbourhood. The Curé of Wespelaer is in England. He was so roughly handled that it is a wonder he is alive. He was prisoner with numbers of others, and they were all sent on in front of the Germans towards the fire of the fort of Waelhem. Naturally the soldiers in the fort imagined them to be Germans, and blazed away, the Germans themselves keeping a respectful distance behind. The Curé made all the others lie down flat and himself advanced alone with a white flag, finally making himself seen and understood. Then they were all taken in and sent off in various directions. I am not sure of the details of the story but he appears to have been heroic beyond words. Well, to return to the Director at Haecht. Eventually a boy in the neighbourhood arrived home (having been liberated, I fancy, because he was too young to serve in the Army for years to come); he declared that he had been prisoner with M. le Directeur for quite a fortnight at some place in Germany, but that M. le Directeur had been removed to another place before he left. That at any rate was something to go upon, and M. Aurelie, the Superior of Haecht, who is herself German, determined to find out what had become of him and have him set free if possible. Authorised by the Cardinal, she set out accompanied by M. Seraphine. First they went to Brussels and made enquiries all over the place there, and were finally told at some office where an account is kept of all the prisoners that he was at Magdeburg. With that much information they set off for Germany in the only train they could get, a luggage wagon which went at foot rate. It was during that cold weather, and they had packing cases for seats. However, they did reach Cologne after endless delay and were advised to go with their story to the Cardinal [Felix von Hartmann] there, which they did. They were very well received, and he seemed very much surprised and shocked at all they had to tell him. They seem to have kept their disgraceful conduct very dark in Germany, and nobody has an idea of the barbarities that are being committed here. He said they were to let him know when they had found the Director and how things were. Of course, their idea was to go straight to Magdeburg, but he said it was wiser to go to the other place where they knew for certain he had been, and enquire there where he had been sent, also they must have a man with them. Mère Aurelie's brother volunteered and—curiously enough—just as they were about to start, he received a letter from a German Curé asking for money to provide M. le Directeur with winter clothes, as he was prisoner in some castle in his parish, and he was doing all he could for him. That was just the clue they wanted, but had it come a few hours later it would have been too late. They immediately set out and reached this place, which is right in the heart of Saxony somewhere near Magdeburg, but I can't remember the name. They went first to the Curé, who told them there were 18 priests in this castle, altogether, and besides numerous soldiers who had been made prisoners. His sister washed the priests clothes herself, for she said she would have been ashamed to give their clothes to anyone else, they were in such a state when they first came into her hands. It is hardly to be wondered at considering that they had all been taken suddenly without having an opportunity of providing themselves with the barest necessities, and they had been weeks en route before they reached their final destination. I think they had a permit. At any rate they were allowed to see the Director who, poor man, was quite overcome when he saw them. The Captain in charge was very civil but not able to give them any information as to what were the charges against him (for the very simple reason that there were none). The Curé had been very good and succeeded in bettering their condition considerably, even obtaining that they should be allowed to say Mass, so that they were fairly well off by that time. But they had had a very bad time of it until they reached this place and been very badly treated, even there they had at first had little to eat but bread and water. The two nuns and M. Aurelie's brother, aided by the Curé, began agitating and writing letters all over the place to obtain M. le Directeur's liberation. As they came back they went to the Cardinal of Cologne again, and he promised also to do what he could. Well to make a long story short—about a fortnight later he arrived here safely, having been freed with 400 others, of whom 16 of the priests who had been with him and the rest civilians, all either too young or too old to serve in the Army. He brought a letter from one of our workmen, whom they would not let go lest he should join the Army, and a Jesuit who was with him was also kept back, because when asked where he was going on his return he said that he had been acting as Military Chaplain and should return to his Regiment. You see there is nothing like agitating, you are pretty sure to obtain something in the end.

December 19, 1914.

Mère Antoine arrived back yesterday, bringing with her your very welcome letters. You seem very disappointed that I did not send the famous letter by Mère Ambroisine but I really was afraid. You know perhaps the story of the Jesuit at Louvain, but in case you don't here it is. Right at the beginning they took all the Louvain Jesuits prisoners and were marching them off to their destination when it suddenly occurred to them to search them. In the pocket of one young Father they found a note book in which he had dotted down the events as they had taken place up to date. Among other things was an entry to the effect that in all wars the library of the University of Louvain had been respected and preserved, but that it had been reserved for the Germans to cover themselves with shame by burning it in 1914. On reading that they immediately called a Council of War, and as a result he was marked on the back with a cross. After marching them on a little further he was led out to be shot, and when the other Fathers wanted to turn away they were forced to look. The Father who was here for the retreat was himself one of them, so you can take this as absolutely certain—in any case I always say so when I relate what is only hearsay, as in the case of the Excellency Von Beseler committing suicide. It appears now that it is not true as his photo with his État Major was in a paper comparatively lately. You can understand that I was rather nervous of exposing two of my own sisters to a similar experience by entrusting them with a dangerous epistle like this. They did get through without being searched, but I had no reason to feel sure that they would when they set out. Coming back, charged with letters for numerous members of the community M. Antoine had a very disagreeable experience. The Germans strictly forbid all carriage of letters and have instituted a most rigorous custom at Antwerp. Only the day before M. Antoine arrived a gentleman was found with two quite harmless little notes upon him and immediately put in prison. Another is already in prison a fortnight for the same thing. When M. Antoine found how it was going to be she took all her letters out of the envelopes and opened them out flat to give them the appearance of a bundle of papers and then put them carefully right at the bottom of her valise. They fell into the clutches of an awful man who turned out every single thing in the bag of one of the novices who accompanied her and thoroughly searched them while poor Mère A. looked on in agony. Just as her turn came another man who had just finished his job took hold of her bag barely in time to save it from the hands of the other. He searched very thoroughly too and took out everything except a book right at the bottom. Had he taken out that book all the letters were immediately underneath—you can picture to yourself her state of mind. All the same such adventures do not encourage one to run any risks—for other people at any rate.

December 20, 1914.

One of the peculiarities of this very questionable mode of warfare is the wholesale pillaging that goes on. I don't remember ever reading of quite the sort of thing that happens here. One of the two things occurs. Either a town is bombarded in which case the majority of the inhabitants depart to save their lives or else in villages the people from sheer fright take to their heels on hearing that the Germans are coming. In both cases the houses remain unprotected and the Germans are able to do as they think proper. Well their usual method is to forward all the good furniture to Germany and afterwards to burn the empty house to save appearances. Naturally, the house being burnt, there is no proof that the contents were not burnt at the same time except the entire absence of any debris, in any case, the people being gone, there is no one to bear witness to the facts of the case. Thus at Wavre Notre Dame everything was gone. They had fireproof cellars in which they had stored quantities of things for safety. All the cellars had been burnt and there were absolutely no ashes or anything. Three of the pianos were gone, and when the two first sisters arrived back, there were soldiers with a van busily charging more. Naturally they protested but the soldiers said they were only obeying orders. They managed to get their own way though by finding the officer and complaining. Had they not arrived when they did I suppose all the pianos would have been taken and then the piano rooms burnt.

One of our nuns who is a native of Malines was shown a photo of her home (an ancient historical building) in absolute ruins, nothing but the bare walls and only part of those standing. Naturally she was very much upset, but supposed that it had taken fire in the bombarding of the town, though once more there were no debris. The father was an antiquarian and had collected from the time he was a boy; he is now an old gentleman well on in the seventies I should think, so that the house was literally crammed with valuable antiquities. A week or two later the brother arrived back from Holland and was thunderstruck when he saw the house. In one of the Dutch papers he had seen views of Malines taken immediately after the bombarding, and amongst others this very building which was merely damaged by bombs and had all the furniture piled up in heaps in front of the house. Evidently it was there ready for transport, and the house was burnt afterwards to save appearances. Here one day just after the bombarding of Malines I heard a great noise going on in the *salle des fêtes* and went to see what was the matter, hoping the German soldiers had received orders to march. On the raised steps at the back stood one soldier, his arms full of pocket handkerchiefs which he was distributing right and left to whoever liked to fetch them. In another place were two other soldiers with piles of natural wool vests and drawers which they were handing round in the same way. Evidently the contents of some shop they had ransacked. At Wygmael, the brother of one of the nuns has a shop for things of that description and had just received a consignment of 300 or 300 pairs (I am not sure now which) of blankets in view of the coming winter, when he had to fly. When he arrived back he found two of the blankets with the tickets still on, on his own bed, which had, no doubt, been occupied by some soldier, and not a single other blanket anywhere. Moreover all the woolen goods had disappeared and in their place the soldiers had left the soiled garments for which they had exchanged them—such piles that a charitable neighbour fearing for the consequences of all that were staying there indefinitely had buried it. At our suggestion it was dug up again on his return, thoroughly washed and made ready for the poor. The poor man, however, has completely lost the whole of his stock in trade, and is only consoled by the fact that the infant for the sake of whom he took to flight arrived safely and is thriving. That reminds me—did I tell you we had a dear little war baby born here in the ambulance? He arrived on the beheading of S. J. Baptist and one of the Seminarists who was staying here acted as Godfather (a fact of which he was very proud), so his minute godson was called Jean Baptiste after himself and the festival at once. But to return to the plundering. Some officer left a letter about by accident in one of the big buildings in Brussels—the Palais de Justice or one of those places. It was found to the infinite delight of the *Bruxellois* [people of Brussels] and proved to be from his wife thanking him for the handsome bedroom suite he had sent her, adding that there was not another to equal it in all the village, and that it was so very much admired. She had, however, still one great desire—a grand piano—perhaps he could manage!!! The villagers all around had seen wagon-loads carted off like that, and what they don't want to burn they want only to destroy, smashing furniture for wood to light fires, etc. People seem to imagine that bombarding necessarily causes fires, and so easily believe that a place was burnt because it was bombarded, but my experience doesn't seem to teach me that at all. On the contrary it seems to me that it is rather unusual for the bomb alone to cause a conflagration unless they use a special kind of shell which they have for that purpose expressly so I am told. Here we were bombarded twice, and the second time all day long, yet the first time there was no question of fire, and the second two small beginnings which extinguished themselves without doing any damage, and one of them was caused by the lighted *veilleuse* [nightlight] beside the dead soldier, on the top of which fell cupboards, doors, etc. Fortunately it was such a small light, and the things which fell on it were so large that they finally extinguished it instead of it setting light to them, though a big hole was burnt in the drapery of the altar. The other was really rather curious. A huge "*obus*" came through the window of one of the classes sideways apparently, for it went bang through the wall at right angles to it into a little long narrow room used by one of the nuns for all sorts of odds and ends, but so narrow that it ought to have gone right through the wall opposite on to the staircase beyond, especially as it had made such a huge hole in the first wall. Well along this second wall was a sort of bookcase with a white curtain in front and statue of our Lady on the top shelf. All around were various papers, a packet of unbound messages and other things of that description. After the bombarding this status was found entirely surrounded by bullets but itself untouched, the curtain half burnt and none of the papers had taken fire. It really was most extraordinary.

2

January 3, 1915–December 29, 1915

January 3, 1915.

BY THE TIME YOU get this it will, I fear, be rather late to offer you my good wishes for the New Year, but still you will have the satisfaction of knowing that I offered them in spirit at the right time though circumstances are against my sending them. Our present masters are getting worse and worse as to the passing of letters, and although there are still charitable people to be found who will run the risk one does not care to be responsible. I hope you will all have read the Cardinal's pastoral letter.[1] Here it was read publicly in all the churches on New Year's Day, and the following Sunday was a day of special Prayer for the Allies as in England and France. I thought the letter splendid, but it was risking a great deal. There were German soldiers in the church both here and at Wespelaer when it was read, and no doubt nearly everywhere else. Next day we heard that both the Cardinal and his printer had been

---

1. *Pastoral Letter of His Eminence Cardinal Mercier Archbishop of Malines. Christmas 1914*. Official Translation (London: Burns and Oates, 1914). Entitled "Patriotism and Endurance," the Cardinal's Christmas letter describes the sufferings of the Belgium people and German atrocities. The words of Mercier were forceful and courageous. According to authors Horne and Kramer, "Mercier saw the calumny against Belgium as one of the country's heaviest tribulations; he roundly rejected the legality of the German occupation and called on his flock to withhold their recognition." Horne and Kramer, *German Atrocities, 1914: A History of Denial* (New Haven: Yale University Press, 2001) 271.

made prisoners, but later on we heard that they had been liberated through the intervention of the Papal Nuncio. You will probably know far better than I how much of this is true, we hear so little and often that little is not correct.

Last week we had a poor woman here to ask for help (we have several every day for food or clothes, etc., the misery everywhere is so great but you can take this case as a specimen). She had been comfortably off and never beholden to anyone for help in her life, 25 years married, a husband, one son, six daughters, and in worldly goods 9 cows, worth about £28 each, a horse for which they had just paid double that, besides pigs, etc. Well the soldiers went off with 8 cows leaving the worst of the 9, also with the horse and all the rest. They burnt down the house and shot the husband and her beloved only son, which was the proverbial last straw. She is left houseless with six daughters and a cow as sole means of sub-sistence. Do you wonder that she is inconsolable? Each time I hear one of these dreadful stories (and they are our daily bread), I feel quite sick. Somehow it is so much easier to love one's enemies in theory or at a distance than when you are surrounded by people who do such dreadful things. The very sight of a grey uniform makes me go green and really feel quite sea-sick, yet those we have here at present seem quite harmless and inoffensive. Elderly men for the most part and anxious for nothing so much as to get home again to their wives and children. However, there seems to be no signs of their desire being realized for a very long time to come. Dora will not know herself when she is next able to pass this way. It is quite useless to describe things. You have to see them before you can form any idea at all, and so much clearing up is going on that it looks almost respectable now to what it was.

January 9, 1915.

I have quite lost my respect for that famous Iron Cross of which they make such a fuss. When the naval doctor got it and seemed so pleased I really thought it was worth having though we were all rather surprised when he said he had received it for his conduct on September 12th, as we could not make out that he had done anything very special and he had spent a good part of his time indoors here. However, we supposed that he must have signaled himself by some act of bravery during the short time he was out and there ended the matter. But when the famous État Major came along, low and behold every single one of them sported an Iron Cross. I looked vainly for a single officer who was not wearing it and could not discover even one—yet these were the previous men who were not to be exposed under any circumstances, who told us that their presence in the house was an assurance of safety for us. Even one of the cook's assistants appeared after two days' absence with an Iron Cross—a really horrid man he was too. I can almost believe that perhaps he had earned it by some act of extra cruelty.

Mère Aurelie in her travels met the officer who took all the Haecht nuns prisoners. She asked him what had been his motive and the horrid man replied that he did it because he enjoyed the fun of seeing how frightened the sisters were.

At one of our convents they had six superior officers to lodge for the night. The following morning one of them came out of his room without a rag of any sort on him and walked up to one of the nuns to ask for hot water. You can imagine her indignation. She turned her back upon him very naturally saying "*Retirez-vous Monsieur*" [Remove yourself, sir] after which the superior took upon herself the supervision of that corridor. Another, or perhaps the same one came out again for hot water, this time I suppose he considered himself sufficiently clothed as he had donned that big cape affair they wear, but he was received in like manner and I do not fancy they got any hot water. We were horrified when the sick officers walked about like that, but they at least had their shirts on underneath which was quite respectable in comparison. I could of course tell you of things far worse than that, but they are utterly unfit for the pen of a religious and I have no doubt that you will have heard much in the papers. We have been most mercifully preserved and have always been able to keep them well at a distance and in their place. That in itself is a thing to be grateful for to the end of one's days. I don't think we can ever be sufficiently grateful to Almighty God for the dangers through which we have come safely. At the time I was so busy in the ambulance and I really did not worry at all and am only learning gradually the risks we ran. That horrid doctor for example who went off with 23 soldiers as prisoners and insisted on taking the 7 German girls back to Germany with him because we were "in very great danger" when pressed for his reasons for saying so tried to get out of it, but we discovered after that he had given orders that the house was to be fired and that it was for that reason that he had first sent away all the wounded Germans and the German pupils. Another time cannons were placed to set fire to the house and a third time a soldier was busy pouring petroleum all round ready when he discovered that it was an ambulance and struck. Some disagreement among officers caused it to be put off, and we were once more saved. Probably there were other times of which we knew nothing. Naturally at the door they kept quiet so that we should not be alarmed unnecessarily, and now details are gradually leaking out. It is not for nothing, however, that we could not undress for days together.

The Cardinal was never taken prisoner after all, only the printer, but the German Governor of Brussels arrived at Archbishop's Palace and interviewed him. He seemed to have been rather taken aback when he found out the kind of man he had to do with. Our Curé went to see the Cardinal the same day and came back with the good news. The letter has caused no end of excitement. All the following day and up till midnight the soldiers were going round to the different presbyteries demanding of each Curé his copy. Many of them had two copies or even more so they naturally made no difficulty in giving up the one they were known to possess. Naturally everyone is doubly anxious now to read it, and it has already been reprinted and is selling like wildfire on the quiet. As it is forbidden to read it in the churches (a few priests carefully misunderstood and not being allowed to read it at Mass read it at Benediction instead it appears), people unite to hear it read in most unlikely places—*estaminets* [a small cafe, tavern] for instance. The Authorities??? couldn't have taken a better method of ensuring that everyone should read it than by taking this action.

Isn't it lovely to think of a Bishop's [Mercier] pastoral being read in general in a public house!!!! People will pay anything for a copy. It was to have cost 2d. but I believe it now costs 5d.—that, however, makes no difference in the sale. If you have seen it you will see with what care he gives the names and occupations of the murdered priests. I see that he says that the Curé of Herent has not yet been found. At Herent they told me he had as I said further back, but perhaps it was a mistake. Then I suppose that the number of priests I gave before were those missing, for many were prisoners or in exile, and nobody knew what had become of them; their whereabouts is being gradually discovered. For ages we thought the priests who had been taken off with the Director of Haecht must have been killed, as we could get no news, and at Antwerp everyone imagined that M. le Vicaire of Borgerhout had been shot at Louvain, but he was here for two months unable to give any news, as we all were. He was stopped by the German soldiers with the two seminarists as he was returning from Louvain and trying to reach Antwerp on foot and sent in here like so many other refugees. The better sort of soldiers seem to have had that much humanity left in them and appear to have thought we were the safest place, though really I don't think it was safe anywhere just then.

January 16, 1915.

The Inspector was here yesterday, and as he came from Aerschot we got some details from him of the horrors that took place there. I told you before that the Burgomaster and his son had been shot. The pretext, as usual, was that civilians shot at the soldiers and as usual it was a got up affair, the shooting being done by German soldiers dressed as civilians. They have done that nearly everywhere. At Aerschot, however, a German officer, who was, I believe, in the Burgomaster's house, got shot by these so-called Belgian civilians, and although the Burgomaster with all his family was at that time in the cellar, he was held responsible and shot with his son. His brother was also shot in spite of the fact that one of the German officers had been with him during the uproar and bore witness to the fact that he had had nothing to do with it. The officer was sent elsewhere and the man shot just the same. He protested, and also against the Burgomaster's murder, saying that he had more than done his duty, having warned the villagers very strongly against using any violence, and that they had only to question them; but it was of no avail; it was evidently a pre-arranged affair like Louvain, and they were shot just the same. The villagers were drawn up in a line and every third one shot. Dreadful, isn't it?

We seem to have been a sort of depot for everyone's treasures and also for all the churches around, destroyed or not. Thus we had here the Blessed Sacrament from the village, from Haecht convent and village, from Wespelaer convent and village, from Delle, from Bueken, from Werchter, from Wackerzeel, and I am not sure where else, I fancy Wygmael too. M. le Directeur went also to Rothselaer, but it was already in safety. Both there where he went and at Werchter where Rev. Mother General went, in a German automobile, the same thing had taken place. The ciborium had been put for safety in the iron safe let into the wall of the sacristy, and a hole had been made in the wall from the other side, the ciborium wrenched out of shape and the hosts scattered among the debris. Naturally, it was supposed to be the work of a bomb in both cases, and in both cases it evidently was not. A German Captain helped Rev. Mother General to collect the scattered hosts and rendered her great services saying that he was a Catholic but had been quite unable to hear Mass that day in spite of its being Sunday, but that now he considered this the best spent Sunday of his life. He was evidently very pleased with himself, and now an old pupil has just sent us a cutting from a German newspaper, an article sent by this very Captain giving a detailed account of it and speaking of Rev. Mother General as his "little nun". It is hardly to be wondered at that the Germans in their own country have no suspicion of what goes on here when their newspapers feed them on such touching incidents as that.

January 19, 1915.

I have just come back from Werchter where I have had the usual pleasure of contemplating numbers of burnt and charred ruins; we passed through Wackerzeell where it is just the same, even worse in proportion, but there the church is in fairly good condition not burnt or desecrated at any rate. As usual quantities of tombs—some soldiers but chiefly civilians, five pairs of brothers amongst others; at Werchter the church is burnt as at Bueken, willfully after the second battle—the following day so that there is no shadow of pretence that it was bombarded. The Belgian soldiers had destroyed the bridge over the Dyle (for the two rivers Dyle and Demer meet at Werchter) and the Germans had constructed a new one so well and so completely that I did not notice the difference until the children drew my attention to it. True I had only been there once before—you remember on my way to Tremelo to visit Father Damien's[2] birthplace; but now that I reflect upon it, it seems to be that this bridge is a finer one than the other, and it is no temporary affair but completely finished off and the tram lines across, everything as though it had always been there. They say that everything was prepared beforehand and that the Germans had measurements practically of every bridge in the country and pieces prepared in case they were destroyed, so that they had nothing to do but fix them. At Termonde they seem to have put up a new bridge in less than no time and perfectly. Since I have seen the one at Werchter I am quite ready to believe it. At Werchter there was a large dairy run by a German, and he is suspected of having been a spy and having given the necessary information. His house was spared by the Germans when they burnt all those which surrounded it, but it got burnt afterwards, nobody knows how or by whom, though everyone suspects his neighbour, and really I can hardly find it in me to blame whoever did it.

2. Joseph de Veuster (1840–89) took the name "Damien" after he joined the religious order of the Sacred Hearts of Jesus and Mary in 1859. He is remembered for his courageous missionary work among the lepers on the island of Molokai.

The newest German craze is cutting down all the walnut trees, they say they require the wood to make guns, but that they will pay for it?? Perhaps with promissory notes on the Bank of Paris as they are accustomed to do. In any case they have demanded the one the Wespelaer nuns have in their little garden. It is the only shady tree they have at all, but I doubt very much if they will succeed in preventing the soldiers cutting it down. During our walk we saw three soldiers sawing one down under the superintendence of an officer in the garden of a house which had been burnt down. They have been to every house to inspect, and I fear that in almost every case the people will let them have their own way from sheer fear. The very idea of our people being forced to give their trees to make German guns.

January 20, 1915.

That letter of the Cardinal's is having plenty of adventures. At Haecht new shirts and chemises were openly given to the poor— wrapped up in each was a copy of the pastoral. One young deacon was en route with a valise full of them with a few articles of cloth- ing on the top for the sake of appearances when he was stopped by a German soldier to enquire what he had in that bag. "Why clothes of course" was his perfectly true answer, and the soldier merely poked at the bag without opening it, so that he got off in safety. At St. Gudule at *Bruxelles* they called on the Dean of the Cathedral to demand his copy of the letter. "Oh, certainly", he answered, "Here it is, but I am afraid I cannot stop I have to say my Mass now". And off he went to the Cathedral, said his Mass, read the letter in public and then distributed hundreds of copies. One Curé having been forced to promise that he would not read it, had it read at every Mass by his Vicaire. Another refused to give it, saying that he had to say his Mass and read it first, and when the soldier protested that he must accompany him to the *Kommandatur* [headquarters, local German military command] said "Afterwards—afterwards". The soldier came back in about an hour, but he still refused because his Vicaire had still to say his Mass, and the letter must be read there too. Eventually he did accompany to the *Kommandatur*—after the second Mass—and they harangued him, it seems, for three hours. When eventually he departed, they wanted to shake hands, but he wouldn't have anything to do with them. In the towns they dare not do much, they are beginning, a trifle late alas, to consider the reputation they are making for themselves in history. The Curé of Herent's body *has* been found just where it was always said to be, 34 other people were found buried in the same grave, women and children among the number, and it seems some very important personages who had disappeared and could not be accounted for. There is a Franciscan friar who is making it his business to exhume the bodies everywhere in order to ascertain what has really become of people and also, of course, from sanitary motives. It was he who had this grave examined and it was also he who came here to place the soldier I told you about in the coffin he brought with instructions from the family.

Those horrid soldiers did cut down the walnut trees after all, but they were not very successful. In spite of all the protests of the Wespelaer nuns, they broke down the hedge of their garden, and then cut down the tree which proved rotten inside and quite useless, though it gave the poor nuns all the shade they have in their garden. However, they are so glad that it is of no use to the Germans that they are almost consoled for their loss. Several other trees also proved to be worm-eaten, or to have a hole or something. They had marked 87 at Wespelaer alone, which they were going to cut down in spite of their owners. I don't know how many they found to suit them. Not many, I hope, but the poor owners have the loss just the same.

Letters, etc., are beginning to arrive. It seems that these are letters which got left at different post offices that are gradually being cleared now. We are always a little surprised that the parents and relatives of the children who were here for the holidays and really in very great danger took it so calmly and made no move, but now the letters are arriving begging and imploring to have them sent at once, etc., etc. Of course it would have been practically impossible to send them in any case had we got the letters, seeing how well we were kept prisoners in our own house. However, the English are all gone now except 4, and we hope that two of those will still be fetched by the American Consul. He came on behalf of the father to fetch one and then again to fetch three, but we gave him five in all, as they had all been asked for. It seems that he promised to come again for the other two who have relations in England. Then we have only Poles, Brazilians, Belgians and two English children whose relatives are in the Cape and New Zealand respectively, and naturally we can hardly undertake that.

May 1, 1915.

There is a somewhat lengthy interval between this beginning and the last part of my letter but thereby hangs a tale. I had thought to have seen you long since, and for over a month had a valise ready packed, waiting in our cell to be able to leave for England at any moment. Mère A. sent for me several times it seems, but her first letters did not arrive; we got one dated January, giving full particulars of everything she said after, only a week or two back, and that enabled us to understand lots of things which had mystified us before. When the first of her letters arrived asking for me it was more or less a complaint that I had not already arrived and the next day, March 18th, two German nuns went to Brussels to procure pass ports but none were forthcoming. They are getting more and more difficult and suspicious. The two nuns apparently were suspected of being spies and found themselves followed about everywhere by three German policemen. However, I was not allowed to unpack as it was always hoped that an opportunity of some sort would turn up but it didn't and when Rev. Mother heard from several different quarters how dangerous the crossing had become on account of the mines, she eventually let me have my own way for once and unpack. Don't imagine for a moment that I am not longing to see you all again for I am, and should be delighted to come to England for a week or so if I could be certain of getting back again at the first alarm, but at the present moment I feel that my place is here. I should never get over it if anything were to happen and I was away.

Nothing at all exciting has taken place lately. On April 9th or 10th I received a letter from Herr v. Mendelssohn Bartholdy [Albrecht Mendelssohn Bartholdy (1874–1936), legal scholar] dated April 1st(How it took all that time to get here from Brussels I can't imagine, seeing that it was stamped all over with eagles and German affairs) he informed me that Violet was enquiring for me as none of my family had news of me since the beginning of the war. Of course by that time I knew that you had seen Mère A. but probably Violet had not received anything you may have sent to tell her so. He told me also that you were all well and Violet and Otto too. He also offered to give her news of me if I was able to write. Naturally I replied at once (in French as he wrote in French) and told him that you had seen Mère A. that we had been bombarded and had had an ambulance, etc. Vague, general and safe news, and then sort of half invited him to come and see for himself if he had the time and inclination. You see as he is such a friend of you all I felt bound to be as civil as possible, especially since he after all was volunteering to offer a service. I have heard nothing since so conclude that either he has not received my letter or does not intend to come, of which I am not really very sorry. I am sick to death of the sight of that dreadful grey uniform. Only this morning I had to accompany an officer to the churchyard to try to identify the grave of a German soldier who died in my *salle*. However we didn't discover much as they have exhumed all the soldiers everywhere and reburied them at a proper depth, Germans and Belgians apart and numbered. I think that the Burgomaster will know where the three we were looking for were, but as three were buried together in one grave without coffins I do not see how they can hope to identify one of them now, after an interval of over 8 months. However, that is their business.

During the holidays we went for some very interesting walks. One to Rothseleer [Rotselaar]. There over 300 Belgians were surprised by the Germans while they were having their breakfast, and 265 were killed. Dreadful, isn't it. It seems that they were betrayed by some girl whom they (the Germans) threatened to shoot if she didn't tell them where the Belgians were. There is a separate graveyard for them with 47 Germans on one side and the 265 Belgians on the other. At Wespelaer there is also a separate graveyard, and at Bootmeerbeck too. I daresay in other places too where I have not yet been, for the fight seems to have extended along the whole region Malines-Louvain, and the number killed seems far greater than was at first supposed. Another day we went to Holsbeek and Kessel-loo. The latter was particularly interesting as the Germans had taken the bricks out of the wall of the churchyard (which is a high wall like the one round our garden) in zig zag all along quite regularly so—and had used the holes to shoot through, being themselves protected by the wall. There were 65 Belgian soldiers buried there and 28 Germans I think. As usual several civilians too. They had burnt the houses of all the people who had harboured the Belgian soldiers or given them anything. At Holsbeek the château was also entirely burnt down because the owner is an officer. It really is sad to see the ruins everywhere.

The night before last 3 aeroplanes were seen and the German soldiers put to guard the railway crossing at Hambosch (our little hamlet on the Canal) were so frightened that they left the railway to take care of itself, and came and passed the night somewhere behind our farm buildings. I heard to-day that they have now paid a Belgian to guard it for them at night. I wonder if it is really true. They certainly are not very numerous and cannot feel very confident but I should hardly have thought they would have thought they would dare to leave their posts like that.

July 5, 1915.

Everything is so desperately quiet in our neighbourhood at present that I do not find much to add to my letter. I made two attempts to write for Dora's birthday. One was utterly unsuccessful as the man who was to have taken it got caught the week before. The other may have reached its destination but in case it did not I will repeat the only interesting thing that has happened lately. On the 6th of June, I think it was, we were awakened quite early by what sounded like a distant thunderstorm but we soon realized that it was not that, as the thunder followed so closely and there was no lightening. We knew at once that it must be fighting of some sort and much nearer than anything we have heard since September. In the course of the day (good news travels fast you see) we heard that several aeroplanes belonging to the Allies had been flying over the three fields where the Germans keep their airships. In two cases they had not been very successful in the bombs they had thrown but at Evere, the most important of the three the success surpassed all that could have been desired. The shed took fire and a Zeppelin, besides 5 aeroplanes were completely destroyed. The people turned out en masse to gloat over the disaster and the Germans were furious confiscating bicycles right and left. The town has had to pay a heavy fine as the water pipes, etc., were broken and also they absolutely had the audacity to rejoice openly. It seems that a Berlin paper explains that the heat in Belgium is so terrific that a shed containing a Zeppelin took fire!!! Besides the affair at Evere (which is a suburb of Brussels in case you don't know) these same aeroplanes on their way met another Zeppelin sailing over Gand. They managed to fly over it and set it on fire, unfortunately it fell on to a convent which also took fire but the Zeppelin was of course completely destroyed, which was a good night's work I consider. At Brussels the Germans are busy having up the pavements in all sorts of places to try to discover how the *Bruxellois* manage to communicate with the Allies. They are furious but can discover nothing. They are also searching vainly for the editor of a certain newspaper, the *La Libre Belgique* which manages to appear pretty regularly in spite of them and which has the cheek to drop a copy in [General Moritz] Von Bissing's [Governor-General of occupied Belgium] (the German Governor of Brussels) letter box. They are wild but naturally their fury is impotent. We had a copy of it here the other day. On the front page was a photo of Von Bissing holding a copy of *La Libre Belgique* in his hand. The photo was entitled "His best friend" and an article explained that it was his best friend because it was the only newspaper that dared to tell the truth so that he was deceived by all the others. The Germans do make themselves ridiculous by all their prohibitions. First it was posted up that no one might sing the *Marseillaise* under penalty of 200 marks, I think. Now in Brussels they may not wear the national colours [black, yellow, red] (fine 600 marks) next day everyone was wearing an ivy leaf which has the advantage of being in 3 divisions and at the same time of meaning "I cling to thee". That was immediately forbidden too. Now they are trying to forbid the teaching of French in government schools, allowing only Flemish—*and German!* The children may not be taught patriotic songs nor in any way be excited against our mild and kind hearted rulers. The schools are liable to be visited by a German inspector at any minute and any infraction will be punished by various penalties of which I believe 2 years imprisonment is the maximum. One poor young man from this neighbourhood a Seminarist, sub-deacon, should have been ordained deacon this time was caught carrying papers for the Cardinal. He was condemned to be shot but so much was done that his penalty was remitted to *15 years* imprisonment, and he was taken off to Germany for *hard labour.* Isn't it disgraceful? They are so mean and petty in their exactions. All the clocks are obliged to mark German time, which is an hour in front of ours. Consequently, at midday the village church strikes one and so forth. However, that worried nobody, for the simple reason that they took no notice but now some young lieutenant inflated with a sense of his own importance has arrived at Wespelaer and has made a fuss because the Angelus is rung at what he calls one o'clock and has insisted that it shall be rung at midday by the church clock, consequently at eleven, under pain of 5 marks each time. So for the last few days we have this curious innovation in the village. His zeal for the ringing of the Angelus is very edifying, is it not! It is like the devil quoting Scripture. He is also trying to insist on private people changing their clocks and the other day an *estaminet* at Herent was fined the 5 marks because their clock marked Belgian time. I wonder when they will try their hand on us for we simply take no notice whatever and ring everything as usual. I have personally no desire to get up at half past 3, because it is half past 4 in Berlin. I suppose as a matter of fact that they are hard up for money and seek any pretext for getting it. Thus the poor Cardinal was fined 30,000 frs. the other day for the ovation he received from the inhabitants of Malines when he set out on foot for Brussels to plead their cause with Von Bissing. They defeat their own ends of course, for he is naturally more popular than ever, and the most noted socialist in Malines protested that it was the town which ought to pay. I suppose you know about Malines but in case you don't here it is in a few words. The Germans insisted on having the former workmen at the arsenal to work for them and posted up a notice for 4 or 5 hundred I forget which. The men naturally did not appear as they had no idea of making bombs, etc., for the Germans, and the latter exasperated posted up a notice to the effect that if the required number of men did not present themselves by a certain day the town would be closed to all traffic, cut off from communication with the exterior, etc. Nobody arrived except two or three men who sat down and did nothing. The German soldiers who were working there encouraged them not to work saying that they would be sent to the front if workmen arrived. The authorities then proceeded to execute their threat. It seems to have had a semi-comic result for the people would not take it seriously and turned everything into ridicule. No vehicles even dog-carts might enter or leave the town so the people pushed them themselves they even invented sending a couple of boys walking about with their heads through the two ends of a ladder the wares hanging from the rungs.

Eventually the Germans gave it up as a bad job. I think they find imposing fines a more satisfactory and profitable job. I could keep you laughing by the hour at the way the people play them off and they haven't the sense to take no notice and pretend not to understand but work themselves up into a rage and bluster and threaten. Thus when the national colours were forbidden three young girls went out together each dressed completely in one of them; a lady and her two children too. All they can do is to fume.

August 15, 1915.

I was very glad to get Dora's letter in answer to mine for her birthday. It was the first time I had had direct news of you since December. Now I have just answered a second letter from Herr von Mendelssohn enquiring about me on Violet's behalf. I have enclosed 4 photographs and a P.C. of the house asking him to send them to V. and she is to send them to Father since you say she writes through Bonnie. I wonder if you will ever get them. As a matter of fact they are really intended for Mère Ambroisine so that she can get postcards of them printed for the old pupils. It has again been a question of sending me to England; this time to conduct a novice for the new convent in Manitoba. It was ¾ decided when another companion turned up in the shape of an English nun from Hythe who had got caught at Vilvoorde by the war. They are anxious to have her back to take a class at Billericay, I fancy and so Rev. Mother General was merciful and let me off. I am not at all keen on the job M. Ambroisine has apparently in store for me. A class of 25 girls to prepare to pass their exams for the London Chamber of Commerce, French, Shorthand, Typewriting, Advanced Grammar, Composition, Business Letters, History (commercial) Geography, Arithmetic, etc. It is all very well but the responsibility of getting them through would turn my hair grey and I have just assured the German authorities that it is brown. Oh, that reminds me. These two were to go to England through the American Consul but had to have a permit from the Germans so they set out for Brussels to get it. Mother Joseph of Hythe had an awful affair. She had come to Vilvoorde for the holidays towards the end of July last year on account of bad health I think. Anyhow, as she didn't really belong there they didn't trouble to have her entered in the registers of the *commune*. When she went to the Germans for her passport they made an awful fuss. It seems that the officer presiding there is a perfect terror. He has lived 26 years in England, has an English wife and is a naturalized Englishman; yet he hates and loathes the English or pretends to and cannot do enough to prove his hatred. Mother Joseph then was treated as a spy, was told that she must be out of her senses not to have had her name given to the Burgomaster and finally was told that she would have to wait at least three weeks while they made all the necessary enquiries about her. The novice was sent back here to get her passport at Louvain. When she arrived there was once more a fuss. "What English: what is the meaning of that? English at Thildonck and we knew nothing about it. We must see into that. Tell the Superior we shall come tomorrow to see about it". Poor Reverend Mother! This was the news brought back to her with various additions in the form of "They looked furious". "We are in for a big fine", etc., etc. Of course we, having no responsibility in the matter thoroughly enjoyed the joke! We counted that we numbered some 25 or 30 guilty of the crime of belonging to belligerent nations. Next day we were put in quarantine. That is to say we were obliged to keep in certain limits and always to have it known just where we were to be found so that their ire might not be increased by being kept waiting. Finally they arrived, 3 of them in a motor, at about 4 o'clock. Naturally when they enquired why our very dangerous presence had not been notified to them, Rev. Mother replied that she had no notion that they wished it. "Why", they said, "there are notices posted up everywhere". Rev. Mother explained that we were not accustomed to go out at all and that when we did so from urgent necessity we did not loiter about reading notices that might be posted up. She might have added especially since those which are usually to be seen at present are a mass of lies from beginning to end. Why one immense thing posted up at Wespelaer and here on the bridge was to the effect that it was not the Germans who had destroyed the churches and public buildings but the Belgians and their allies!!! However, discretion is the better part of valour so she said nothing. Fortunately we are all properly inscribed at the *maison communale* [town hall] and had been overlooked by the Burgomaster. He had replied to their enquiries that there were no foreigners in the village, not thinking of the convent so fortunately we were not really in fault. They took a list of our names, ages, etc., and said they would return during the week to bring the necessary papers and get our signatures, meanwhile poor Rev. Mother had to

sign a document rendering herself responsible for our correct conduct towards the Germans. She had to undertake that we should
do nothing which could prove detrimental to them and that we
should not go any distance greater than from 18 to 20 kilometres
without their special authorization. So after being prisoners all
day we never showed ourselves at all. Two or three days after they
did turn up with papers and then we had to appear but not having been warned it was a regular case of hide and seek all over
the house, not to mention that 2 of the guilty parties were giving
class at Wespelaer and the Germans had the pleasure of going after
them. We had each to sign 2 cards. Blue for the English, yellow for
the French, orange for the Russians. On them was to be found our
name, date and place of birth. Place of residence, profession (mine
is that of *Klosterschwester* [a member of a women's religious order]
in case you feel interest) size, colour of eyes, hair and beard any
special signs or peculiarities by which we could be recognized, etc.
They had to take our word for the hair. Little Mère Paule remarked
that she fancied hers must be white at the present moment. I asked
Rev. Mother if I couldn't give mine in as red but she wouldn't let
me. On the whole we thoroughly enjoyed the joke of finding ourselves so dangerous to the German empire but I fancy poor Rev.
Mother must have felt very relieved when they were safe out of the
building. Now I can no longer extend my walks to a distance of
more than 20 miles which, as you can understand, is a continual
sacrifice particularly as at the present moment we have only one
child here for the holidays and there is no question of walks at all.

September 27, 1915.

Since then M. Gonzague has come back with 4 other nuns from
Hythe of whom one is a little English lay-sister, destined for the
Indian Mission. About the three Belgians there was no trouble
but no end of difficulty for her and the little English sister to pass
the frontier. She has to go through endless formalities and was
undressed twice over, first at the frontier and then at Antwerp.
During the lay-sisters' retreat three Germans arrived once more

to enroll these two new dangers to the Empire. M. Gonzague was forthcoming but the little sister who did not understand Flemish and consequently made her retreat alone was nowhere to be found. You know what it is in a house like this. Over an hour was spent hunting for her while these gentlemen? waited with what patience they might. Eventually she was found sitting quite calmly in the Novitiate.

This last week once more we have soldiers here. A few officers lodged in different houses. Curé, doctor, etc., and dirty wretched looking men, camping out with dirty wagons, camp kitchen, etc. They are forbidden to say whence they come and are under orders to let it be thought that they have come from Russia. Apparently they have even been carted about the place in trains for several days and nights so that the length of their journey may convey that impression also. But—they smoke French tobacco—pay with French money—are able to describe the condition of Lille and Arras but have no knowledge whatever of the climate of Russia nor of the condition of things there. One or two of the men have been got to talk and admit that they come from Arras where they have been badly beaten and obliged to take to their heels. We are all hoping that this is true for they had been boasting (not these but the few we had here already) for weeks past of the great offensive they were preparing and the wonderful things they were going to do. There seemed to be some truth in it for the number of trains that passed was something awful. There seemed hardly to be a pause between them and the people who live close to the line said they were full of men or munition for the most part. We are hoping now that this is the grand result of their famous offensive. Anyhow, we are continuing the novena to St. Michael with great fervor.

I am not able to find means of writing to you any more. My last method has fallen through like its predecessors. It seems that the English authorities have stopped it as the Dutch intermediary was suspicious. If such is the case I am more than resigned for I would not for the world procure my own personal satisfaction at the expense of our troops. After all, the success of the war goes before everything else.

October 2, 1915.

This morning great excitement. Almost immediately after breakfast several Germans dressed as civilians arrived in 2 motor cars which they stationed before the *externat*. Four or five arrived here and the others directed their steps toward M. le Directeur's house. The first I knew of it was hearing men's voices speaking loudly as I was going along a corridor in the cloisters. I looked up in my astonishment and beheld Rev. Mother coming along followed by three men. She proceeded to conduct them upstairs which added to my amazement. Just then two other sisters came along and told me to follow as those men were Germans and they did not like Rev. Mother to be left alone. Naturally I did not wait to be asked twice. They went straight to her room and insisted upon examining everything—drawers, cupboards, registers. They would not allow any of us in the room so we fetched a German nun and she stopped while we remained near in case of emergency. It seems they did not discover anything very special for Rev. Mother is very careful, but they found several letters from Mère A. fairly recent to their great dismay and then they found several of those blank sheets of paper like the one I wrote to Dora on. With those and a few papers of a like description they made a packet and then enquired if we had no printing press. Naturally they said no, but that we had several typewriters and duplicators so they insisted on visiting my establishment. (On hearing that they were in the house, needless to say my first care had been to hide this very comprising epistle). I was just on my way once more to see what they were up to in Rev. Mother's room when I met M. Marguerite coming along with one of them. She said they were coming to visit my room so of course I went too. The man began his visit and started by laying his hands on two or three patriotic hymns in Flemish which I had printed for the poor schools and neighbouring parishes. By that time Rev. Mother had arrived with three others and they began to ransack drawers and cupboards. I felt pretty well at my ease as I fondly imagined that I had nothing that could interest them and had not had time to reflect much. All of a sudden, I saw one of them with Dora's letter in his hand. Her answer to my birthday letter. They were very upset and asked one another how it was possible for letters to get in still. Then they found the famous letter from Daddy opened in England by the censors and two or three lines effaced. Once more they talked to each other and drew attention to the ticket of the English censor. Then they found a letter I had written giving you a second time the Dutch address you once used, but which had not gone as there was no longer means that way. I am sorry they got that as it might get those people into trouble, but they can hardly follow them into Holland. They went off with those and a few other papers after asking several times if we had no other printing press in the house. We thought we were well rid of them when an alarm was raised about M. le Directeur whom they had put bodily into one of their care. It seems that they presented themselves at his house demanding to be given a pistol which they knew was buried there. There really was one it appears but how they could have known it without treason of some sort is a mystery. They then proceeded to visit his house and papers with a zeal that augured no good. Everything was turned topsy turvy. Waste-paper basket and coal scuttle examined, linen shaken out. Every tiny scrap of paper read. They went off finally with the Director and a lot of papers, but we know nothing for he was not allowed to come here and warn us and what I have just related we have learnt from his servant. A few minutes after a neighbouring priest arrived here and he was dispatched post haste to Malines to let the Cardinal know. Now we are awaiting developments. I can't say we feel particularly comfortable as only last week the priest who preached our retreat was carted off to Germany for 10 years although apparently there was not sufficient evidence to condemn him. I have heard since that it was for giving 10f. to a young man to help him to reach the frontier. The case of Delle was more cunning. He somehow got wind of the fact that the Germans were on his track and managed somehow to get away in time having procured a passport beforehand so as to be ready in case of emergency. They have been two or three times since to try and find him but he is safe in France so they can look as much as they like. We are now anxiously awaiting any news that may be forthcoming of M. le Di-recteur. I dare not say even here what I fear lest they should ever get hold of this and find out something from me. I wouldn't get him into trouble for the world nor any of our Allies.

October 3, 1915.

M. le Directeur did not come back yesterday so this morning M. le Curé came at a quarter to six to give us Holy Communion and at about 8 o'clock came here to say a second Mass for which of course he had to have a special permission. The Cardinal sent a message it seems that M. le Directeur would *probably* be back last night or this morning, which I suppose means that he would take steps in the matter. Not knowing quite what papers they found in M. le Directeur's house we don't know quite what to expect, but I am prepared for the worst. The funny thing is that it didn't seem to occur to them that being the Mother House we had the Superior General here and since they made no enquiries we did not think it necessary to enlighten them on the subject, otherwise poor Rev. Mother General would have had her room ransacked in the same brutal manner and we have no desire to have her upset again.

December 3, 1915.

I am making a fresh start since I have had to get rid of the last journal I wrote for your benefit. It is now 2 months since our amiable masters went off with the poor Director, and he is still in their clutches. For a fortnight or more there was no means of getting access to him; he was what they call "*au secret*" [in solitary confinement] and nobody was allowed to see him at all. The supe-riors, of course, moved heaven and earth on his behalf, and finally managed to see him in the presence of a German officer. That was better than nothing, but of course very unsatisfactory. He is in the state prison at Brussels, but under fairly good conditions. That is to say the food is relatively good, and he is allowed to have whatever parcels are sent to him after they have been minutely examined. For weeks there was no attempt at bringing him up for judgment, but finally some moves have been made and the German nuns have been sent for to Brussels where they apparently were made to take their oath not to reveal anything that was said to them or about which they were questioned. They were allowed to see M. le Directeur in prison, and did not give a very glowing account of his state of health. So far, we do not seem to be much nearer to getting him back than we were two months ago, although they make no end of promises. First it was "in another fortnight perhaps" then "in a few days", but the fortnight and the few days have gone their way and there is no sign of the Director. For six weeks he was not allowed to say Mass, now they have managed to get permission for him to do so. The poor man was so overcome that we wept the first time he enjoyed his new privilege. For a fortnight we were helped by the village priests but they already have Delle on their hands as the Curé is in exile (he departed suddenly because he was warned in time that the Germans were after him for having helped young men to leave the country to join the army). One day we had no Mass at all. Then a young professor at Louvain volunteered his services. He cycled here every evening after school hours and had to cycle back in the morning in time to begin his class at 8 or half-past. That is all very well in summer but in November and December it is impracticable. It was pitch dark morning and evening. The roads are none of the best at the best of times but in the pelting rain they are awful and we have now a *Père Prémontré* [a priest, a member of the Order of Canons Regular of Prémontré] who is to stay here until M. le Director's return. He is very kind and devoted—a young man about 35 I should think, and the white habit is very picturesque.

A week or so back all the nuns belonging to belligerent countries were once more sent for to go to parlour. There was a German soldier with a long list with all our names, etc., etc., and we each had to sign a declaration that we would not leave the house between 9 p.m. and 7 a.m. German time which means 8 p.m. to 6 a.m. for us. Naturally we all took it as a huge joke since we are not at all accustomed to take constitutionals at that moment. The man explained to Rev. Mother in a rather apologetic manner that he would be obliged to see that we kept orders and that from time to time he would arrive to see if we were all there. He added that he quite understood that such precautions were superfluous in our case and that we could easily obtain an exemption if we wrote to headquarters. Rev. Mother took it as a joke and told him he would find it hard work to make himself heard here after 8 o'clock as the outer gates were closed very early and there was no bell so that he would probably have the pleasure of trying to climb over the railings. We thought no more about it, but I think they did write to our "*bien-aimé Gouverneur General*" [beloved Governor General] as the *Libre Belgique* calls him, but he is far too great a personage to bother to reply in less than three weeks if he condescends to answer at all. Last night I was sound asleep when at 10 p.m. eleven o'clock German time, someone knocked violently at my door. Of course I thought one of my neighbours must be ill and requiring help but no—"The Germans are there and all the French and English nuns have to present themselves so hurry up" were my instructions. There were two other English nuns in my corridor so it was a nice commotion. When we got downstairs nearly everyone had assembled for most of the dangerous people sleep on the other side of the house and had been called before we were. There was an officer and two soldiers. The officer had the list and a German nun helped him to mark us off while the two soldiers stood at attention in the background. Naturally poor Rev. Mother had been called up first of all to let them in. It was really killingly funny and the scene was worthy of a Kodak which unfortunately was not forthcoming at the particular moment. All the same it is most annoying. Fancy poor little Mère Paule being hauled out of bed like that, and there is a little French nun just her style and age, they make such a dear little couple when they are together as they usually are at recreation. Then several others are delicate and ailing so that it is really most inconvenient to put it mildly. To console us they say that they will probably make a nocturnal visit every week at different hours of the night according to the orders they receive. However, all the inconvenience is not ours. They went first to the farm and of course couldn't get in. Then they went to the front of the house and banged on the railings until they managed to wake one of the nuns who sleeps on that side of the house and who held parley with them from the window. Then they had the further pleasure of cooling their heels for twenty minutes or so while she dressed and went to wake Rev. Mother, etc. Then when they did gain admission it was only to make a further station while everyone was being called and getting dressed. It took them about an hour and a half before they had finished and then it seems they had to go on to Herent which is an hours walk from here, to go through the same performance there. They must bless their superior officers I should think.

December 4, 1915.

They evidently have their eye on us altogether. Two or three days ago a soldier arrived with a summons to the *Kommandantur* at Brussels for a young girl who is here. She is a Russian Pole but no more a Russian than the German Poles are Germans. They are all of them Poles to the backbone, and hate their masters whether they be Germans, Austrian or Russians. She was here as a pupil until the war broke out but quite grown up and a budding postulant, so when the other Poles returned home she remained on I suppose hoping to enter as soon as the war was over for Rev. Mother will not accept postulants as long as the war is on. Well, yesterday she went then to Brussels (she had to whether she liked it or not since the soldier made her sign a paper saying she had received the summons) and when she got there they calmly told her she was expelled from the country and must be gone in three days. She begged for a week at least in order that she might be able to let her family know but they said she would get there alright without warning the family, and three days is the limit. She has to take 200 marks with her for the expense of the journey and when she protested that she hadn't got it as of course she hasn't any means of receiving money from her family she was told she had only to see that she got it somehow; in other words the convent has to provide it. Cheek isn't it? The papers didn't come in time after all so Vanda had her week but, not expecting it, had not warned her family. From explanations given to one of the German nuns it seems that some member of her family with a position under Government had requested that she might be sent back. For any case there was a great fuss altogether. Her papers were not in order because being a boarder she was not inscribed at the Maison Communale before the war and the Burgomaster would only vouch for her "*sous réserve*" [with reservations].

December 23, 1915.

When the papers arrived it was with instructions that she had to have crossed the frontier by a certain day and was to go straight through to Warsaw without leaving the station when she had to change. We have now had a P.C. from her so I suppose she has arrived safely at her destination.

We had a second nocturnal visit 5 days after the first but as they arrived an hour earlier than the other time they did not find the house quite so fast asleep and managed to get in more easily. Also, being prepared for the emergency we did not take so long to grasp what was the matter and amused ourselves by arriving in all sorts of impossible costumes, arguing that anything was good enough for the Germans. Poor Rev. Mother was nearly doubled up with laughter as we arrived one by one. This time they did not think us worth an officer but contented themselves with two common soldiers. They have no photographs nor any means of verifying whether we really are the persons we are supposed to be and it would be the easiest thing in the world to present different nuns each time if Rev. Mother wasn't so dreadfully scrupulous. A second letter has been written to Von Bissing's adjutant this time, protesting. Now two answers have arrived. Von Bissing has deigned to reply (now that the three weeks interval necessary to sustain his dignity has elapsed) graciously releasing us from the obligation of receiving nocturnal visits in future on condition that

Rev. Mother renders herself responsible for us. Almost immediately after came a letter from the less elevated and consequently more polite adjutant saying that the matter had been attended to and the necessary notice was being sent to the local authorities. To make quite sure, however, we wrote ourselves to the officer at Wygmael letting him know that we could be left in peace in future. In spite of that two or rather three days later at 4 a.m. arrived a carriage and a pair containing a superior officer, who announced that he had come to control our presence once more. We don't get up till 4.30 a.m. so once more a grand upset and poor Rev. Mother hauled out of bed but this time she wouldn't have us disturbed but presented her papers expressing herself very much astonished at their further annoyance under the circumstances. The officer, a superior officer this time, made profuse apologies but had received no notice on the subject and had come from Louvain instead of Wygmael so that our letter had had no effect. However, we hope that now we are really going to be left in peace during the night at any rate. We are inclined to think that it is really a kind of personal vengeance to vent upon us their annoyance at Mr. le Directeur's delinquencies. There is a convent [male community] of French Assumptionist Fathers at Louvain, all under 60 and consequently not allowed to return to France because they are of age to carry arms. You would think they were far more dangerous than a handful of women wouldn't you? Well they have had no trouble at all nor had to sign, nor had visits nor anything, and it seems that nobody in Louvain has been bothered at all, nor have we yet heard that any of our other convents have been disturbed. Yet we should be almost certain to hear if they had.

The poor Directeur is in prison—12 weeks on Christmas Day, and so far his judgment has not taken place. I am almost glad, as from all that is said it may be worse after than before, but we shall see.

A week or so ago the brother of our Burgomaster arrived home to find the Germans making a careful search in his house. They were there already half an hour, and were carefully turning the pockets of his clothes inside out when he arrived on the scenes.

He was suspected of being in communication with the front, but they found nothing at all suspicious expect one unsigned letter, which of course was as good as nothing. He protested that he was quite innocent simply because, being the father of four motherless children he was on his guard for their sakes, but that except for them he should have been at the front long ago. They immediately enquired where were the other two, as they only saw two little boys, and upon being told that they were here at school, the Germans replied "Ah that is a regular"—well I suppose in English we should say wasps' nest or robbers' den or something of that kind. We feel quite flattered, for until this affair of M. le Directeur we had the reputation of siding with the Germans, etc. for the simple reason that that was the only motive that people seemed to find that could account for our hair-breadth escapes of having the houses burnt about our heads I don't know how many times.

December 25, 1915.

Needless to say how much I think of you all, but I can do nothing but pray and hope that all is well since it becomes more and more impossible to get or send letters. We had a grand excitement last night. Being Christmas Eve, fast, vigil, big silence, etc., we were all packed off to bed early in order that we might get up earlier this morning for the solemnities of the day. We were barely in bed, lights out, etc., before there was a grand commotion, people running about, voices, etc. A thing quite unheard of after night prayers when all is silence and recollection until after Mass next morning. My first idea was that it must be the control officers once more in spite of our exemption, and I felt anything but pleased, though it struck me as rather curious that they didn't knock at my door. However, in a few minutes someone called out that M. le Directeur had arrived and lights were turned on. Everyone arrived at the door of her cell in some particularly picturesque costume to assure herself of the truth of the statement and to enquire what was the correct thing to do under the circumstances. Finally we decided that the best thing to do was to make ourselves respectable and go down to welcome him after his 12 weeks' captivity. The ideas of what a respectable appearance is proved to be very varied, and as we arrived down one after the other we had great fun at each other's expense. We found the Directeur in Rev. Mother General's room with Rev. Mother, M. Assistant and such sisters as had arrived there before we did. Some of us certainly presented a very grotesque appearance, but indeed we were picturesque when compared with the poor Directeur. He is a very dark man at the best of times, but the brown "leathery" skin, as Dora calls it, had become sallow from want of exercise, and he had a growth of certainly 3 days if not more, beard and moustache on him. The result was dreadful, you really would not have troubled him with the tongs. His hair too was all lank and long. He really was a most disreputable looking object, and looked so tired too, poor man, only of course overjoyed to get back again. You never saw such excitement as there was, his return was so utterly unexpected. We had practically given up all hope, for although everything possible had been done, the last excursion on his behalf had been so very unpromising in its results that we had quite made up our minds that if he was ever judged he would be packed off to Germany. There was not even a bed for him in his own house.

December 29, 1915.

Yesterday he had a grand dinner when all the priests in the neighborhood came to congratulate him on his return. He has not quite settled down yet, and says he has hard work to realise that he is a free agent. However that will soon wear off I think, for he is having a week's holiday; we are keeping our "Père" on purpose, and he does practically nothing but receive or pay visits. What a queer lot those Germans are to be sure. The uncle and two brothers of our Père were shot at Aeschott [Aarschot]. When the Germans arrived they drafted off the women and children to the Grand Place where they were compelled to remain standing all night; they were not allowed even to sit on the ground. They heard a great deal of shooting going on, but could see nothing of course. Finally, the next day they were allowed to return to their houses, but naturally could find no signs of husbands, fathers, brothers. When they were bold enough to make enquiries, they were told that they had been taken to Germany, and it was not until six months after when the bodies were exhumed that the truth was known. The poor men had been made to dig their own graves and get in and then were shot down. One group was exterminated, another group every third man. The third brother of our Père with a friend of his managed to make their way up to the top of some shop into a room full of empty packing cases and hid in two of them. Some soldiers had seen them and followed. They pierced as they thought all the cases with their bayonets, but by an all-merciful providence omitted to pierce three—the two in which these poor men had hidden and one other. Wonderful, isn't it? They escaped eventually by the roof. This, of course, is comparatively ancient history, dating as it does back to the beginning of the war; but somehow it comes home to one more when one sees the people to whom it all happened. The more I hear the more I realise how much we have to be grateful for. Only a few weeks back I had a traveler here trying to obtain an order for paper, etc. He remarked that we had not suffered at all, and when I said that we had been bombarded twice and that the house was dreadfully damaged, etc., he said that was not what he meant. He meant that we had not been taken prisoners, or hurt in any way or pillaged. I said that the reason we had not had the house pillaged at all was because we had remained in it to protect our belongings, whereupon he laughed and said that that didn't make much difference. He then related to me what had happened to the Brothers of the Christian Schools at Paxy Fogennes [Passy-Froyennes]. They were his best customers and he had often spoken to me about them. They have an immense boys' school and numbers of typewriters, duplicators, etc. Well, the Germans arrived. First they took 14 of the Brothers prisoners, then they proceeded to cart away all the furniture. After that they installed their troops bringing typhus with them. The mortality was such that the orchard and kitchen garden were converted into one vast cemetery, and now the poor brothers can get no pupils—naturally parents are too frightened to risk their children there.

3

March 13, 1916—November 18, 1916

March 13, 1916.

This is a long interval, isn't it? But there is really nothing to say and it is so doubtful if you will ever receive this at all. There seems to be practically no safe way of writing to England, and there is no means of hearing either. Of course there is always means of risking dangerous methods, but Rev. Mother doesn't like it, for there is very little doubt that we are very carefully watched over since this affair of M. le Directeur. Before that the French nuns used to get occasional news of their families through a Dutch lady or rather a Belgian living in Holland, who received letters for them and then wrote the contents on postcards which she sent as coming from her. Now nothing from Holland ever reaches us except by accident, so we conclude that the Germans suspected that there was something up, though I really don't see what harm it can do them for us to know that our families are well or ill as the case may be.

Lately we have once more had a rather disagreeable officer down at Wespelaer. (It does make such a difference who is in command). The results was that all those who had to go anywhere were obliged to furnish themselves with a *"carte d'identité"* [identification card]. On New Year's day some of the nuns from Haecht tried to get here, but were stopped at the station at Wespelaer and sent back again because they had no card, and that in spite of the fact that one of them was herself a German (we gloated over the last item naturally). The funny part of it was that one of them really belonged here and had only been sent to Haecht to help for a few weeks, so that she could only procure her card from the *commune* here. On the strength of that all those who teach in the poor schools or go out for walks with the children had to be photographed and supplied with cards. That makes my second. First the blue as a subject of a belligerent country and now a yellow one like the common of mortals. Some weeks after the Rev. Mother had to go to Haecht, so she tried to bring back poor Sr. Felix in the carriage. Going all went well and nobody stopped them or made any enquiries, but coming back of course the carriage was stopped at the station and they had no end of trouble to persuade the wretched man to let Sr. Felix pass. They did manage it eventually. A few days later they heard at Haecht that this officer had been changed, whereupon the very next day they arrived here without any cards at all quite at their ease, saying that nobody would worry about them now which proved to be correct.

Everything is getting fabulously dear because we cannot get the necessary things from outside. The Germans too are making all kinds of rules and regulations, house to house visits, etc., nominally to control the quantity that each possess, so that everyone can have sufficient, but in reality we think to furnish Germany and their troops at our expense. We are constantly having soldiers here to enquire about something or another. On two successive days it was to see what provision of potatoes we had, and they insisted upon visiting cellars, etc., another time oats, another flour, another pigs, etc., etc. You have never finished with them. Now an order has arrived that nobody may kill a pig without a permit, and then it has to be taken to Louvain and killed at the "*abattoir*" [slaughter house] there. Another that each village has to supply one cow a month, or a week, I forget which, to the Germans. But of course it is all in our own interests, and but for their "wise precautions" we should all have died of starvation long ago. It is beginning to get pretty serious. In the towns food has been a vexed question for a long time, and it is gradually getting worse and worse, even in the country. Meat is hardly to be had for love or money, so that there are several Fridays in the week from sheer necessity. I can't say that it troubles me much personally, as I am neither superior nor a lover of meat, so that I have not to worry about other people or about myself. But it must be a very anxious time for poor superiors. Naturally the hatred of all that is German increases with each fresh difficulty. The children never speak of the Germans except *cochons* [pigs]. They enquired when we were out the other day if I had my *passe-cochon* ["pig" travel pass], meaning, of course, my passport, and when we were taking the names of quadrupeds the other day in class, they would not accept a pig as a quadruped, because they maintained that at present they went about on two legs. The Germans are pretty cool too. They give themselves such airs and one would think everything belonged to them. We are constantly finding German soldiers walking about at their ease in the garden as though it was a public park, and one went so far as to come with a camera and take views without asking anyone. Naturally he was politely asked to take himself off as soon as he was discovered. Yesterday there were two walking about like fine gentlemen; they were also shown to the door, but one cannot keep a sentinel on the watch all day long.

On the other hand there is a perfect fury for everything English. Everyone is made to learn English, and the children, who were always so troublesome in class before, now never have enough. The great idea is to be able to talk to the soldiers if ever the Allies come this way. Everything English is quite perfect and delightful? It is really quite funny. I am getting quite tired of perpetually teaching my native language, for the nuns are even worse than the children, but there—it doesn't do to be selfish, and it is better to encourage affection for the English than the contrary for the Germans, isn't it?

March 28, 1916.

Now they are afraid of the other countries too. A few days ago they arrived to enquire what subjects we have belonging to neutral countries. We used to have several Dutch nuns, dear old Mère

Cecile being of the number, but all have died 2 during the war except Mère Emmanuel who is almost constantly in the infirmary and doesn't leave her room for months at a time. We have nobody belonging to other neutral countries except 3 little Brazilians and an Armenian in the boarding school and for a wonder children don't count. Well they tried to insist upon seeing M. Emmanuel, but finally had to give way as there was no question of taking German soldiers up to interview her in bed. They had the *garde-champêtre* with them (a local functionary who corresponds more or less with our village policeman) and he maintained that he remembered M. Emmanuel quite well, which was probably quite true as she was *portière* [doorkeeper at a convent] for so long and he is charged to keep a strict watch upon her as she may not leave the house under any circumstances and he has to come every three days to assure himself that she is still here. To do him justice he does not take the matter too seriously for he has not been near the place since and quite right too. Poor thing she cannot even get as far as the Church for Mass on Sunday and she is going to become a danger to the German Empire. It seems to me that it is after all preferable to belong to belligerent countries for we at least may go a distance of from 18 to 20 k.m. [kilometers] during the daytime while the poor neutrals may not go out at all. We have only to be reviewed about once a week and have obtained an exemption from that and they have to show themselves every 3 days. I wonder what our amiable governors will invent next.

June 16, 1916.

Another long interval and now I am ever so sad at feeling the 21st so near and no possibility of writing to Dora for her birthday. It becomes more and more difficult and I have no longer the courage to worry poor Rev. Mother about my own personal desire for news from home when there are nearly 30 others in the same state and she has such difficulty in getting business communications from M. Ambroisine. I ended up "I wonder what they will invent next". Well, here is the latest invention!! There are no end of men still left in Belgium. Many who have never served their term of service under the old military law and others who were not old enough when the war began but are now besides those who were in ill-health, etc. The Germans are naturally most anxious to keep these men under their own eye for fear they should manage to find their way across the frontier and join the Army. They are forced to sign an agreement not to leave the country, they have to present themselves to the G. authorities every month and besides their families are threatened with heavy fines or imprisonment if they are not forthcoming. One poor lady lately discovered that in spite of all her precautions her son barely 16 years of age had managed to give her the slip. When he had got safely out of the country by some method best known to himself he sent her a P.C. to say so. In the midst of her distress she received a visit from the Gs. demanding a fine of I don't know how much with the alternative of a month in prison. Protests of her utter ignorance, etc., were quite useless so like a plucky patriot, she refused to pay a penny and spent a month in prison instead where it is to be hoped she had leisure to console herself for the loss of her son. All of this is a digression however, so I will return to my personal experience. During Office [Divine Office, the public prayer of the Catholic Church. Professed religious, such as nuns, are required to recite the Office daily] on Tuesday evening Rev. Mother suddenly disappeared and when we came out on our way to Benediction she was at the door as if waiting for somebody. She made signs to several to follow her which seemed strange and then began to laugh saying "*Oui venez*" [Yes, come along]. Then it suddenly dawned on me and on everyone else I fancy, that the Gs. were there once more to control us. We arrived at parlour escorted by Rev. M. General and Rev. M. thinking it a very fine joke. The first who presented herself came out half amused, half indignant saying "Why he asked me my name, my age, and if I was quite well. Whatever has that got to do with him". But with each it was the same so that it soon dawned upon us that there must be method in this new madness and that he must have some reason for this third question which seemed so uncalled for. We decided in our own minds that if they had their eye on us as being dangerous we were less dangerous ill than well and that consequently it would be wiser to parade our small ailments than to hide them. No. 1 for instance had replied in her astonishment "*Oui Merci Monsieur*", and as a matter of fact she suffers agonies from liver complaint. Another half crippled with rheumatism had done likewise. We persuaded the latter to return and I went in at the same time. He (for there was only one) seemed quite glad and hunted for her name on the list marking rheumatism against it and then he said to the Rev. M. "it is easier if they are a little ill" which seemed to me queer and suggestive, but although I could not conscientiously plead ill myself, I took good care to warn all those that followed to make the most of any ailments they might happen to have.

In the evening Rev. Mother explained that the Gs. wanted to oblige us to present ourselves every month and that for the last three weeks they had been "moving heaven and earth" to get out of it for us pleading that several were old, sick or delicate. This man it turned out was a Doctor sent to sift the truth of these statements. He really seems to have been rather a good sort anxious to do all he could to dispense as many as he could, no doubt realizing as few Gs. seem capable of realizing how very disagreeable it would be for us. Thus one nun who is very pale naturally arrived and he at once said "you are anaemic" and without waiting for a reply marked her as such though she really is not at all ill. Needless to say she was dispensed. Two who were ill in bed he refused to visit saying that the shock might do them harm. Quite decent for once. We must give even the devil his due. Finally he departed saying he would do his best but that we should have to present ourselves at Haecht on the morrow unless he heard to the contrary. Rev. Mother was most anxious we should not go and seemed convinced that all would be well, but next morning during Mass a notice arrived dispensing all but six of us and Maud Leon [?]. He seems to have given in as incapable of the walk to Haecht and back (which really is pretty considerable 50 minutes each way) all those over 50 whether they pleaded ill or not and all those under 50 for whom he could find any reasonable pretext. But we others had to go whether we liked it or not. On the road we met about 20 youths going in the same direction, but even that did not quite prepare us for what was coming. When we arrived we perceived the road in front of the gendarmerie black with men; the court yard in front ditto the passage to the side door idem [the same]—and what was worse they seemed to be patiently awaiting their turn. We very quickly made up our minds that that was no place for us and that the sooner we got out of it the better, so that we would risk trying to pass through and get attended to at once. It was a true case of nothing venture nothing have, for they let us through them without a murmur. Inside it was just the same the first room packed with men and on the other side a second entry was blocked with heads and finally another room full of men all lined up (in alphabetical order I fancy) taking their turns with three soldiers writing away and several others on sentry duty. We marched bravely up to the top as though we had every right to do so, and were attended to on the spot though the soldier in charge didn't appear to have a very clear idea of what he had to do for us, and finally contented himself with stamping the date on each card, whereupon we departed as fast as we had come. Even the man who was being attended to when we arrived made no difficulty and two other ladies—one the French Governess of two of our children—the other the English lady's maid of the Countess at Wespelaer—who had been waiting already half an hour—followed at our heels and passed with us to their great satisfaction. There must have been several hundred men there and not one said a word, though they seemed extremely interested in us, but then they were Belgians and Catholics so that they must have realised themselves that it was no place for nuns. How the German authorities can have the face to oblige women to face an ordeal like that I cannot think. As we passed the schoolmaster who was standing at the door he tried to encourage us saying "never mind it is a nice walk anyhow." *"Vive les allies!!!"* Rev. Mother doesn't mean to let us go again, if she can help it but if she doesn't succeed in procuring an exemption for us we shall have to go the second Wednesday of every month.

The following day M. le Directeur went to Brussels to get back his papers. He had written to protest that he was in difficulties for want of the papers they had taken when searching his house and had received notice that he could fetch them on the 15th. He went through I don't know how many portfolios but did not get everything back though he did receive a good deal that he was wanting. They wouldn't give him the papers belonging to the convent. I suppose they expect us to go ourselves if we want them but from what I can make out he must have come across Dora's last letter sent a year ago by the "*Petit mot du soldat*" [underground mail service]. Alas! This year there is not much chance. When he had finished he enquired why they had put him in prison in reality. They tried to make out that he knew, but he maintained that he had never had a definite explanation so they explained thus:—You were put in prison to represent the Covent of Thildonck, just as M. Max [Adolphe Max, Major of Brussels] is in prison for the town of Brussels and you had a very narrow escape of being sent to Germany. Your convent is *Anti-German* and you had to be taught a lesson as well as the villages and others over whom the convent exercises an anti-German influence. We had thought of taking the Superior General but she is a woman (aren't they getting humane all of a sudden) and suffers besides from ill-health, so that it was scarcely possible to take her and there was no one else to take—they are all women. (They haven't put any women in prison yet—nor sent any to Germany,—nor shot any—they are quite incapable of such things) so we took you instead. You are the Director and represent the convent so you were made responsible.

Had you heard the applause when we understood that the authorities considered us to be anti-German you would have almost inclined to think that there was something in it. They further added that after all he had nothing to complain of as it was almost an honour for him to have been in prison. Almost indeed!! The point is that they had no right to place him there although it was a great honour for him.

June 21, 1916.

To-day it is Dora's birthday and I am sure she still hopes against hope that something from me will arrive sooner or later, but alas! As for father—I have not been successful this year. We are altogether queer about the time of day. Early in the year the Germans gave out that for economical causes all Europe was going to change the time making everything an hour earlier during the summer months. They were already in advance of us and oblige all the public clocks to follow German time, so that at Wackerzeel where there is a sundial on the tower of the church as well as a clock, the dial marks 11 when the clock strikes 12 and so forth. On a certain day everything was to be changed an hour which would bring us to German time. Whether it was really true that other countries were doing the same or not we are unable to judge having nothing but their word to go by, and that has no longer any market value. Anyhow, they changed too perhaps because they were convinced that otherwise people would stick to their own time in spite of them and now we have a curious phenomenon that when the village clocks strike 12 ours strike 11 and in reality it is only 10 o'clock, it is queer to say the least of it.

October 23, 1916.

My journal gets on very slowly because I only add to it incidents that are likely to interest you whenever you read it and also that I can vouch for. So much talk goes on that if one kept count of all one hears it would never end and so much proves to be untrue afterwards. At first I believed all I was told thinking that people would not relate as facts things of which they were not morally certain, but now I am very slow to accept as a fact. However, here is one story which I have every reason to believe. It was related to me by the girl's uncle. You will remember that I told you earlier in this letter how I had to go to the cemetery to verify the body of one of the soldiers who died in the ambulance. Well, a few weeks back his father who is a doctor at Liege was here for the requiem which was sung in the village for the souls of those soldiers killed here. All the villages round about were bombarded at the end of August or the beginning of September 1914 and each village has a solemn requiem sung on the anniversary of the fight. This Mr. Dury left Liege at 2 a.m. to be present and, as I happened to be "*Bon Pasteur*" that week, it fell to my lot to see that the poor man had some breakfast. It was rather a fortunate coincidence as I had looked after his son for the 2 or 3 hours that he lived after being brought here and had identified the body after so that I could give him more information than anyone else. (By "*Bon Pasteur*" we mean the sister who stays away from Mass and Benediction to answer the door if necessary. We take it turn and turn about for a week at a time and everyone is delighted when their turn is over). He was very full of all that had happened and was happening and this is what he related to me while he was having his breakfast. He had three sons and his brother has also three. All the six at the war. His second son who was doing his year of service when the war broke out was killed within the first month. The other two presented themselves as volunteers with their father's consent. He added that if he had had twelve sons he would have let them all go. One of his brother's sons is a prisoner in Germany. All the four remaining have been wounded at least once but have returned to the front. One curious incident was that the Commandant of his second son one day congratulated him for some act of bravery and told him that he should recommend him for a decoration. He had hardly finished speaking when a shell burst close by and all the company, Commandant as well were killed on the spot. The only two who escaped apparently were this lad and his cousin both of whom were wounded. Now for the story. At midnight some German officers (or soldiers I don't know which) presented themselves at his brother's house saying they had come to arrest his daughter aged 23. They said that they came at that unheard hour from a feeling of delicacy as it would be so disagreeable for a young girl in her social position to walk through the town with bayonets on either side in broad daylight. Naturally she would have felt rather proud on the contrary whereas it was most disagreeable to be alone with those men at midnight. As a matter of fact I expect they did it to avoid the ovation which she would most certainly have received and perhaps also to render her position awkward. She was accused of having helped the French soldiers at the beginning of the war which she frankly admitted saying that she made a point of helping anyone in distress and did not feel in any way obliged to enquire who they were. The father asked why he was not arrested saying that his daughter had done nothing without his consent and approval and that whatever she might have done he had done far more, but they merely shrugged their shoulders saying that their orders did not mention him. The girl then was taken away, and lodged if I remember rightly in three different prisons finally being brought back to Liege. All the time she was kept in solitary confinement, "*au secret*" as they call it. The father refused to have her defended. He said it was merely playing into their hands and he proved to be right in the long run. At last after 73 days she was brought up for judgment at 5 or 6 a.m. After several hours she was taken back to her cell and then a German—very *chic* and *distingué* [distinguished]—speaking perfect French—presented himself. He said that he had been present at her trial and had made himself thoroughly acquainted with all the details of her accusation. That he was moved with pity for her extreme youth and offered himself to defend her. He told her that her position was practically hopeless—that she was condemned to be shot early the next morning. He questioned her in every possible way (always in her own interest) and said that, in spite of all he could promise to obtain her acquittal or at any rate a mitigation of the sentence of death if she would avow the least little thing. She seems to have been pretty plucky for she told him that she told him that she had nothing to own and that her death would be merely a further crime to add to the list of those already committed by the Germans but that they were so hardened that no doubt a murder more or less did not make much difference to them. Finally this "gentleman" withdrew, and left her to her reflections and to prepare for death as best she might. A few hours later he came back and returned to the charge. He begged and implored her with tears in his eyes to have pity on herself—on her family, etc., etc. He said that if she would merely state that her silence was to prevent others being betrayed he would still manage to save her, but she said she was very much obliged to him for taking so much trouble, but had nothing further to say and turned her back on him so that he was obliged to retire without having obtained any satisfaction. At *1 a.m.* she was sent for once more by the judges who informed her that she was condemned to 3 months imprisonment and that as they were over she was free—and they turned her out into the streets there and then. She discovered that 30 odd persons had been arrested at the same time as herself and treated in much the same way but that they had all allowed themselves to be entrapped like that into acknowledging something or other on the strength of all these fine promises and that all had been condemned to from 10–15 years of penal servitude in Germany. She was the only one who got off. Aren't they dreadful!!

November 7, 1916.

The children are in retreat so I profit of a few free minutes to continue my diary. Some weeks back the Vice-Consul of America came to enquire for all the English nuns. He was quite a young man and was sent by the Consul to assure himself or rather to reassure us as he had been told that we were uneasy on account of all the fuss that the Germans keep making. He came in a motor car after office hours to gain time I suppose and brought his young wife with him. She was quite charming and the cousin of one of our old pupils. He insisted on seeing us all and assured us that we had no cause for anxiety as long as we were not caught committing one of those acts which the Germans call crimes. Thus the Père who is preaching the children's retreat is only lately delivered. He was a year in prison because he gave 10 Germans [German currency?] to two young men to help them to cross the frontier to join the Army. This is qualified by them as treason because we are (in case you shouldn't know it) Germans and consequently any act committed directly or indirectly against the German Government is treason to our *"Patrie"* [homeland, country]!!! The poor father, who is over 60, was kept for two months in a soldiers prison at Louvain in a cell so dark that even at midday it was impossible to read so that all that time he could not say his breviary. Then he was taken with numerous other prisoners to the station. They were packed like sardines into a Black Maria [police van used to transport prisoners] with real criminals. The father was next to a German sentenced to four years penal servitude for theft. He was in three different prisons in Germany and is expected to consider himself very leniently treated with only a year's imprisonment when he ought to have had from 1–4 year's hard labour for the crime he had been guilty of. They were made to sleep a great deal to make up for the insufficient food. Every day they went to bed at 7 and got up at 6 while on Sundays and feast days they had to get to bed at 5 and get up at 7—only 14 hours sleep. The method of ensuring that they did so was ingenious to put it mildly. They had to fold all their clothes and place them outside the door of their cells on a bench—caps shoes and stockings everything. Naturally having nothing but a shirt to put on they had no choice but to go to bed. He described the diet to us. Poor man what he must have suffered and there were over 300 Belgians and Frenchmen— all civilians with him—two or three over 80 years old. This is a digression—to return to the Vice-Consul. When he had satisfied himself that we were not really alarmed he asked if his wife could see over the house and jumped at the offer to accompany her. They appeared to be charmed and stayed for quite a long time after-wards. He volunteered to make enquiries about any members of our families who might be in America but he could not undertake to send any letters. There were so many who asked that I thought it would be abusing of his kindness to ask him to make enquiries about Bonnie and family especially as they are in Canada and not U.S.A. Eventually they went off in their motor laden with grapes for themselves and the Consul and seemed to be as pleased with us as we were with them. They begged us to be sure and let them know if we were molested in any way and promised to pay us an-other visit after the war.

Towards the end of September Rev. Mother was obliged to go to our two convents of Wolverthcim and Londerzeel to make some arrangements. She set off very early in the morning to get the first tram because it takes so long to get anywhere now. No one will use the train if they can possibly help it because it is German and the trams are so slow and inconvenient.

As they approached Hever with its famous Zeppelin shed the tram suddenly stopped and everyone was made to get out. There was an aeroplane flying overhead (some people say there were several but Rev. Mother only saw one) throwing bombs to try to destroy the shed. They took refuge in a cottage close by feeling none too safe there and after a time things seemed to have quieted down and the aeroplane had disappeared so they got into the tram once more and went on a little farther. Once more the tram came to a standstill and this time it was much worse and there was absolutely nowhere to shelter, not a house to be seen. They had a most awful time. We heard the explosions here. The aeroplane had returned to the charge and the Germans were pretending to try to bring it down with their *mitrailleuses* but what they really did was to use shot that only exploded when it reached the ground so that it was the poor harmless civilians who were killed—six people in one family. I think there were 20 or 30 killed in all and several wounded but I can't remember exactly the number. A young girl from Wygmael was among those killed. She had been in service in Brussels for just a month and was out with her mistress when she was struck. I suppose the idea of the Germans is that if the allies see that it is the poor Belgians who pay the price they will give up attacking their installations. It seems to me a very cowardly way of doing things but I have got to that stage at which nothing astonishes me, from them at any rate.

Poor Rev. M. arrived safely home again with nothing worse than a new war experience and a good fright you can imagine how thankful we were to see her again safe and sound.

At the beginning of October a gentleman presented himself at the residence of the Ursulines at Lierre. I say the residence because that is one of the three houses which have been burnt down.

Most of the nuns are in England where they all took refuge when they were bombarded but a few came back with Mère Assistant to continue the poor school which, being at a short distance from the convent had escaped. The superior fortunately for her, is here as her health is so bad and the shock as you can well understand did her no good. Well these nuns manage to exist and make both ends meet as best they can very courageously. It was early in the morning the first week in the new school year and the nuns were just ready to set off for the church with the children for the "*Messe du Saint Esprit*" [Mass of the Holy Spirit] which always inaugurates the school year when this gentleman arrives. He said that he was a Mr. Parmentier and professed to be a great friend of certain members of her family of whom he gave her news and also of many of the sisters who had remained behind in England. He said that he had to do with the Belgian Government and gave her all sorts of information which she knew in other ways to be perfectly correct so that she allowed herself to be completely taken in and quite at her ease, and gave him all the information he wanted. He stopped for half an hour or ¾ so that the other nuns were obliged to set out for this Mass without her. At the end of that time he stood up and said "I am not Mr. Parmentier at all. I am a German officer and you can repeat all you have said in Germany". He thereupon left the room locking the door after him and enquired for the Superior. Naturally the M. Assistant appeared as such since the real Superior was not there and could not be held responsible. He went with soldiers and ransacked the cell of this M. Augustine and then went off taking with him M. Assistant and M. Augustine. You can imagine the consternation of the other nuns when they returned from the Mass. He also took a little servant girl and her father. They were all taken to Brussels to St. Gilles where M. le Directeur was for 12 weeks last year and there they are still though we have done everything possible to get them released. Nobody knows exactly what they are accused of. It is certain that they managed to correspond with the nuns in England and they are said to have had something to do with the *Presse Française* which is a sort of newspaper which appears on the quiet without the German censure I believe, but really I am not quite sure and still less so as to whether they had anything to do with it in reality. One of the Wavre nuns was also put in prison because she received a letter from her brother who is at the front and it came to their knowledge. But she was only kept a fortnight and has been set free again.

November 18, 1916.

We have, as you know, several French nuns here and some from the same community are at Laeken, another of our convents. Naturally they write to each other whenever they can manage it and pass on any interesting news they may have. A few days back the Laeken nuns entrusted a parcel for our nuns to a linen-draper who lives near the tram asking her to give it to anyone she knew to be coming here. She seems to be a very obliging sort of person and often sends us things from Brussels in that way. She volunteered her services some years back out of pure love of the Ursuline habit I believe for she was educated at one of our convents and really we have much reason to be grateful to her. Well, she was awaiting the desired opportunity when a gentleman? entered and demanded the parcel for Thildonck. She refused to give it to him saying that there might be things of value in it for all she knew and that she would not entrust it to a total stranger, whereupon he went to the door, blew a sort of policeman's whistle which he had and two soldiers arrived. She had no choice poor thing but to hand over the parcel and to accompany these three worthies to the *Kommandantur*. There she was kept for several days though of course she was perfectly innocent and had no knowledge of the contents of the parcel. It might have contained groceries or medicines or anything else of the kind for all she knew to the contrary. A week later the Germans arrived at Laeken and enquired for the two French nuns concerned. They visited their cells, made them turn out their pockets, etc., etc. They seem to have spent from 2 p.m. to 5.30 inspecting their cells, etc., but so far have not taken them to prison. Naturally, we are hourly awaiting our turn and expect a second perquisition at any moment. We are wondering what will be the result of it all. What possible harm there can be in writing to each other even if they do occasionally express themselves in terms somewhat uncomplimentary to the Germans I cannot see.

There is much smothered excitement and indignation at present over the men who are being transported to Germany. The Germans of course say they are only sending the unemployed in their own interests. That they are giving them well paid work and good food (if the food in any way resembles what they gave the poor father in prison I am very sorry for them). The point is that they cause the men to be unemployed by forcing the factories to close. Thus at Louvain they may only have one place for cigars, a certain number of breweries, etc., consequently all those existing unless authorized by the Germans are obliged to turn away their hands who are immediately seized upon as being unemployed. There is some talk of their taking the others too but I don't know if they really will. There is talk of taking them from 15 to 55 years old but we hope it will come to nothing.

Now about the state of things generally. I imagine that I had related to you how the Assistant and Mère Augustine of Lierre together with a young servant and her father had been taken off to prison at St. Gilles in Brussels, where M. le Directeur had the pleasure of spending three months. Well the judgment was finally given and the M. Assistant was allowed to depart as there was not sufficient proof of her guilt.

4

June 28, 1917–December 28, 1917

June 28, 1917.

M. AUGUSTINE, WHO HAD of course betrayed herself was condemned to 10 years hard labour and the other two with her. They
have all three been taken off to Germany and are there still. I don't
know exactly in what the hard labour is to consist but they say it is
the making of uniforms for the German soldiers.

Some weeks back we had a few hundred soldiers in the village for the night. They imagined they were going to stay for several days but were ordered off next morning. We protested that
we could not possibly lodge men in a convent and they actually
listened to reason and contented themselves with sending a dozen
horses to the farm to be stabled. Two or three men came with them
to take care of them, but they seemed to expect nothing better than
to sleep on the ground by the side of their beasts. They were quite
grateful for an old palliasse which was given them. And so meek
and quiet—very different from those of three years ago.

The great excitement at present is the requisitioning of the
brass and wool. All the brass has to be given to them (don't they
hope they may get it) and they are going to take the mattresses too
for the wool. They say that it is for the soldiers' uniforms but I don't
know if that is so. Anyhow they have already visited Louvain for
the brass and we are expecting them here any day. You can imagine

the anxiety of M. Parle. We are expecting refugees from the North of France and Flanders any time. Campenhout and Relst an hour from here have some already.

September 2, 1917.

The brother of one of the nuns lived at Menin quite on the frontier. For three years he and his wife had the use of an attic and the kitchen. I think the rest of the house was occupied by three officers and twenty three stationed in the factory. Finally they were made to leave with the other inhabitants of the town and were only able to take with them a few absolutely indispensable objects, a mattress and clothes for themselves and child with the layette of the baby expected in less than a month. They were dropped down at the village outside *Bruxelles* where they were under police surveillance, in a strong family and forbidden to leave the village although they knew nobody there and had relatives willing to receive them at Antwerp and at Charleroi. Finally they have got to leave to come here and have hired Marie Schodt's house. Naturally they will never see any of their belongings again and all their fortune was in kind as they manufactured organs. After all theirs is only one case out of thousands.

There was a grand visit for the brass a week or two back. No end of soldiers came to the different villages round and everyone was expected to come and bring what brass they possessed or at least to declare it. Each family had besides to declare what land they had and with what it was planted and how much it produced. Their statements were to be verified afterwards with exorbitant fines if they were found to be untrue. They came here but were not admitted (only two came). They were told that we could give nothing but that if they liked to take it by force that was their own look out. I suppose they didn't feel in a position to do that for they said that they had no orders to do that but that we should do very much better to give what we had and not lay ourselves open to imprisonment and fines which would certainly result. So far we have heard nothing further but there is time yet, so we are waiting to see what will happen next. M. Rufine's sister-in-law was here the other day. She lives at Tarnhout and always has an officer with an orderly quartered in her house so that she can hide nothing. They have taken absolutely all the brass she has even the handle of the front door and the brass plate round the bell, the knobs off the drawers of tables, etc., and the officer pays nothing at all but if she refused him anything on the plea that she hasn't got it he sends his orderly to buy it and she has to pay the bill. These are some of the many advantages of High Culture and German occupation. The price of everything is fabulous, an egg for example is any price from 6 ½d. to 8d. or 9d.

December 28, 1917.

In October our refugees arrived. First a community of 50 Franciscan nuns from Roulers whom the Cardinal [Mercier] asked us to house so that they might be able to continue to live as a regular community. Their convent is entirely destroyed by bombs. They brought with them two or three old ladies and several other seculars. They have quite settled down now and seem very contented with the way they have been received. One of them had a paralytic stroke on the way here and had to be transported on a stretcher, she is gradually recovering the use of her limbs but will always remain more or less paralysed on the left side. (She has died since). At the same time as these nuns arrived we received our contingent of refugees. There were about 12–1,500 destined for Thildonck, Wespelaer, and Velthem, but by some mismanagement the whole lot were sent to the convent here when they arrived by train at Herent, which is an hour's walk from here. They arrived there a little after 3 a.m. and began to arrive here at about 6 o'clock. It was pouring with rain and they had to come on foot as every available conveyance was needed for the luggage. Orders had been given that all the horses, oxen, dogs, etc., with their carts had to be at Herent at midnight to receive these people. You never saw such misery. They came in groups wet through, tired out and hungry, hoping for beds, firing, and food, but of course it was utterly impossible to house such a number and the committee had only supplied soup for the 500 expected here. It was dreadful. Families with 5 or 6 little children, babies a few weeks old, etc. The people were nearly all of the very poorest class from the back slums of Menin. We had to manage as best we could. They were placed in the 3 big *salles* and there they had to hugger mugger [remain in a secrecy or in a clandestine manner]. It was quite ten days before they managed to find lodging for everyone and meanwhile we had them here sleeping on straw in the *salles* and we had to serve out three meals a day. You have no idea the work it was for such a number and the state of the *salles* was something awful. Several were ailing or had wounds of one sort and another (for they have been bombarded off and on for the last 3 years) and they had to be looked after as well as the circumstances permitted. At last room was found for most of them. Three families are lodgers in the farm and fifteen in the poor school. The children from the poor school came here for class until there had been time to put roofs, doors and windows to the numerous houses in the village which were burnt down at the beginning of the war, then these poor people can go into them.

There has been a second visit for the brass. We were obliged to deliver up a certain quantity to escape having the house visited throughout and then nothing escapes. In most of the houses in the village they contented themselves with making an inventory and saying what must be delivered in three months' time. The next event will be for the mattresses and after that the sheets. They seem determined to leave nothing behind them when they go if they ever do, which I am beginning to doubt.

I think I told you that we had a sort of normal school [a training school for future teachers] here since the war. Some of the young girls come from neighbouring villages on their bicycles as the walk there and back every day is too much. At first the Germans granted passports for bicycles fairly easily, but they suddenly put a stop to it and ordered all the pneumatic tyres to be given up by a certain date. Only postmen and doctors were excepted. It was useless to say you had none as they had so carefully given passports so that they had the proof in their hands. One of the *normaliennes* [a student at the normal school] did not give up her tyres on the stipulated day, indeed she came here every day for another month on her bicycle and finally she was called up before the authorities and condemned to pay 100 marks or else undergo 4 days prison. Naturally she chose the latter and presented herself at the prison, she imagined she had to occupy but they sent her on to the women's penitennary at Louvain. There she was told she could not be received unless conducted by a German. Nothing daunted she went into the street and stopped the first soldier she met asking him if he would be kind enough to take her to the prison. The poor man was naturally very much astonished he said that it was not exactly part of his functions but that if she really wished it, etc., and finally she managed to get taken in like that. Naturally the nuns and *aumôniers* [chaplains] were very nice to her when they fully understood the situation but she had to occupy a cell under lock and key for the 4 days and undergo all the other pleasures of solitary confinement. At present it is the "grand chic" to go to prison for a time.

5

February 20, 1918–December 17, 1918

February 20, 1918.

SOME WEEKS AGO I had to take one of the nuns to Louvain to undergo a very serious operation. It was to take place at 7.30 or 8 a.m. on Monday morning, but no professor arrived to perform the operation. We thought it very queer and finally his assistant went to his house to enquire and received as a reply that he had gone to Brussels! on Saturday afternoon, was due home on Sunday evening but had not arrived. No doubt he had lost his train and would probably be home by midday. We waited and waited but no professor arrived and finally at about 2.30 we gave it up as a bad job and returned home very vexed but fully expecting to receive a letter full of abject apologies. Nothing came and at least we heard quite by chance that he was in prison. He had been sent for by a Doctor in what they call the "*Étape*" (the part of the country so near the line of fire that nobody may come or go without a special permit) to perform an urgent operation. He applied for a passport but didn't get it and the doctor at the other end sent a telegram for him to come at once so he decided to risk it. Unfortunately he was caught and sent to prison as well as the doctor who had sent for him. It was 10 days before he was able to persuade them that he was not a spy. He is a very celebrated Surgeon and there is practically nobody to replace him as so many young doctors are with the army.

April 9, 1918.

Since I wrote this the Curé of Delle has been shot as a spy, with 5 companions.

September 30, 1918.

It has been a great shock to us all as we had hoped against hope that they would make it penal servitude for life and that the war would speedily come to an end. From their point of view I fancy he really did deserve it, for he is supposed to have rendered no end of help to the allies. In prison he was most edifying and all of his companions (some of them were the reverse of pious) made their confession to him. He asked as a last favour to be allowed to say Mass on the day of his execution and to sup the night before with those who were to be executed with him. He said his Mass and preached his last sermon, after which the six were taken off to be shot. They refused to have their eyes bandaged and apparently the soldiers were very much impressed with their *sang-froid* and pluck. It seems very sad that six brave men should lose their lives like that but of course they knew what was before them if they were caught and acted with their eyes open.

You will see by the dates how erratic I am in continuing my journal. I really have very little time now that I have the pharmacy and the infirmary. There are always plenty of sick folk to look after and all sorts of unexpected things happen in a charge like mine while I fill in all my odd moments of what would otherwise be leisure at the pharmacy.

It is so long since I last write anything that I am sure all sorts of interesting things have happened of which I have forgotten to keep note. The Germans have now been for the wool. Nobody may keep their mattresses; they have to give the wool to the Germans and fill the sacks with sea weed instead. The hospital at Louvain has had to give all the wool too and the sick are on the same bedding as everyone else. They had to work all night for ever so long to make the exchange so that the poor unfortunate creatures might have beds to lie upon.

Another little adventure! A fortnight ago one of the sisters received notice that she had to present herself at the *Kommandantur* the following day, failing which she would be subject to a heavy fine and prison. Nobody could imagine what was the matter and poor Mère Amelia was in a dreadful state of mind. However, there was nothing for it but to go, so it was decided to send her with Mère Marguerite, one of the German nuns, in the hope that if things went wrong she might be able to set them right. When they arrived at their destination they were told that the official who had sent for them was already at the prison and that they must go to him there. More frightened than ever they set out for the prison and the first thing they saw was two unfortunate prisoners in masks with nothing of their faces to be seen, merely two holes for the eyes. They were washing the floor of the corridor at the entrance. This was not particularly reassuring either any more than the narrow cells on either side with tiny little grated windows high up in the walls. A horrid looking man received them at once came to business accusing M. Amelia of treasonable correspondence and insisting that he held the proofs in his hands. She absolutely denied it saying, that she wrote to no one except her mother here in Belgium and a sister in Holland. Yes Holland that was it—here was a P.C. and he held it up at a distance but refused to give it to her. Fortunately she is long-sighted and at once recognized it as coming from her little nephew aged 11. He said that he had had two prizes at school and that he had been moved up a class—the Germans had taken it to come from a soldier at the front and to mean that he had two decorations and had been moved up or rather received his promotion. It was quite useless to argue, the man was determined to be right at all costs and poor M. Amelia was in terror of being sent off to a cell there and then in spite of her perfect innocence. Fortunately just then another official, more amiable and reasonable then the first arrived and he appeared more ready to be convinced. They had to give the name, address, ages, etc., of family in Holland and it came out that the brother-in-law was being surveyed because he had so much correspondence. No doubt he profited of being safe in Holland to help all his friends in Belgium to keep in touch with their friends and relations. Eventually after no end of assurance from M. Marguerite and protestations from M. Amelia they were allowed to go and receive a huge document to sign swearing that this small boy who had caused all the trouble was really M. Amelia's nephew and as such was entitled to write to her. This was to be forwarded to the censors of the post in Germany to put things straight. They arrived back in the evening with nothing worse than a fright, but we are all on our guard not to run any risks of that kind.

October 1, 1918.

The war continues indefinitely but the British Government have turned up trumps. They look after their subjects as no other government does or probably can. The Dutch Consul is charged with us and if in need they supply us with 80 francs a month besides which doctors, medicine and clothes are also given gratis to British subjects. There is a huge depot at Brussels where everything necessary can be had and in case of illness they will even give 100 francs a month. Royal isn't it? It seems that this had been done all the time of the war only we have only heard of it quite lately.

I told you that the Curé of Delle was shot didn't I? His poor parishioners had been deprived of his presence for over 2 years and left to the charity of neighbouring priests so that they were sighing to have one of their own again. Shortly after the tragedy a new Curé was nominated. He was Vicaire of Werchter about an hour's walk away. In time of war it was impossible to have a cortege, etc., such as I described to you some years ago when our new Curé was installed but these poor peasants imagined a most practical way of showing their joy. Every conveyance in the village went out decorated with branches of trees and flags of all colours to fetch his furniture. Each one set out when he thought proper independently of his neighbour so that the procession began at about 5 a.m. and lasted till evening. There were so many carts and so little furniture that the return journey was most amusing. A huge hay cart for instance with nothing inside but a rabbit hutch another with a chair, a table, or some other article of furniture, a hen or two, etc. Each cart with one object inside so that nobody need be disappointed and the new Curé had his moving done free-gratis for nothing. He at least must have felt that he was welcome and very much desired by his new parishioners.

M. Augustine of Lierre has been liberated. Unfortunately I was in bed with Flu when she arrived but I saw her for a short time the next day. She seems to have had some experiences of what the Bosches are like. One thing she related in my presence was that they (the prisoners) got to hear that they were going to be made to work at the munitions. One Sunday morning when all the prisoners were assembled in the prison chapel a French and a Belgian lady suddenly stood up and said "Friends we are going to be put to work at the Munitions. It is our duty to refuse to resist till death". They were at once silenced but they had done what they intended. Every prisoner refused and the Germans were obliged to desist. The two culprits were so terribly punished that both died as the result of the treatment they received. M. Augustine was afterwards sent to Vilvoorde and it was there that she was liberated but she heard from other prisoners in Germany how those who remained there had been set free. Several hundred German soldiers, deserters, were prisoners close by and when the revolution broke out in Germany they turned round on their warders, and joined the revolutionaries. The first thing they did was to go to the men's prison demand the governor and force him to give up the keys of the prison. Thereupon they immediately set all the prisoners free and any jailor who attempted to interfere was rolled from the top of the stairs to the bottom. Needless to say, they didn't interfere for a day or two. They didn't like to interfere with the women but eventually they made up their minds and repeated the process in the women's prison. M. Augustine was there with the Princess of Croy and lots of other women French and Belgians.

I didn't dare to explain to you how carefully the brass and wool were hidden for fear of my letter falling to alien hands and then they would have had the proof that all had not been given. Naturally the possibilities of hiding in a building like this are unlimited and in all humility I must say that we made the mos‘ of them. We gave practically nothing saying that the children had their own mattresses and took them with them (which was a fact for some of the Belgians and it is quite superfluous to give too many details under such circumstances) and that every soldier transported to Brussels from the ambulance had been carried away on his mattress (It was unnecessary to add that the Germans had brought quite a number of mattresses stolen from the barracks here so that it worked both ways). The French colonel who was here the other day said that what had struck him most in the trams was the delight of the people at having been able to "do" the Germans and hide wool and brass successfully. One woman was openly boasting that she had hidden her mattresses in the forest of Soignies. It so happened that we spent midday recreation unearthing bolsters [a long, narrow pillow] and mattresses, so he was brought to see that particular *cachette* [a hiding place]. He seemed to enjoy the sight immensely and did not consider that he had paid his five hours visit too dearly by a voyage of 5 days. I could tell you endless stories of the way the Germans set to work to discover the brass when they found it, it was almost always due to treachery or jealousy. Thus one family at Antwerp were betrayed by a rival in trade (the German officer himself told them so) and had five soldiers breaking down walls and ceilings for two days until they showed them the rest themselves to prevent further damage but they were practically ruined over it.

Some other people I know saved their mattresses by giving the soldiers who discovered them wine which was in the same place. The soldiers could not make up their minds not to accept the wine offered and so pretended that they had found nothing so that these people, more fortunate than many others saved their mattresses and most of their wine.

December 14, 1918.

As there is a wee piece of white paper here, I profit of it to tell you that this was written for your pleasure and not to give information to the newspapers. It was written at odd moments under all sorts of difficulties, often at long intervals with no sort of attention to composition. I have just re-read so far to see if all is accurate and can vouch for everything, I fancy, except the details of Tamines and the condition in which they found the bodies of the Curé of Beuken and the Père Hollandais. I didn't see them myself nor speak personally to those who did, because I don't talk Flemish and everyone round here does, besides which I was too busy at the time to have much leisure for collecting information. Later on I visited the two graves with the children, but that did not give me any proof as to the condition of the bodies underneath. As for Comines, what I said about the family, of the child who came here is absolutely certain, but the other details I heard here and there, so that they may be inaccurate. You couldn't possibly publish a letter like this so badly composed and so irregular. Besides I know M. Ambroisine has it in her head to get together all our experiences and write them down in some form or other. It would be well, therefore, to keep this for reference later on, as I find on reading it through that I had quite forgotten certain incidents related therein.

December 17, 1918.

The greatest—rather wicked—pleasure I have felt for a long time was a few days back when I was in Antwerp. The tram stopped and quantities of German soldiers, prisoners, marched past in perfect order guarded only by two Belgian soldiers. We were told that they were going to work at the rails, and that often a regiment of them was guarded by one soldier. That is tit for tat with a vengeance!